Studies in Child Development

Able Misfits

Studies in Child Development

The National Bureau for Co-operation in Child Care

Able Misfits

A study of educational and behaviour difficulties
of 103 very intelligent children (I.Q.s 120–200)

M. L. KELLMER PRINGLE

LONGMAN
in association with
THE NATIONAL BUREAU FOR CO-OPERATION IN CHILD CARE

LONGMAN GROUP LIMITED
London
Associated companies, branches and representatives throughout the world

© *M. L. Kellmer Pringle 1970*
All rights reserved. No part of this publication may be
reproduced, stored in a retrieval system, or transmitted
in any form or by any means, electronic, mechanical,
photocopying, recording, or otherwise, without the prior
permission of the copyright owner.

First published 1970

SBN 582 32447 5 Paper edition
      582 32446 7 Cased edition

Printed in Great Britain by Spottiswoode, Ballantyne and Co Ltd
London and Colchester

Contents

Foreword

By Sir Cyril Burt, M.A., D.Sc., LL.D., D.Litt., F.B.A.

'Britain', said Sir Robert Blair, when introducing the London County Council's scholarship scheme, 'was the first nation to recognise the importance of making special provision for the education of her ablest children: it must be our aim to do this regardless of distinction of wealth, influence, or social class'. That was sixty-five years ago. Today his claim may sound extravagant. But both its truth and its relevance to present conditions could be amply justified by a glance at the history of education in various civilised countries throughout past centuries. And perhaps the best way to introduce Dr Kellmer Pringle's interesting studies of gifted children will be to sketch, quite briefly, the historical background of her subject. This too, I hope, may help to forestall certain popular but mistaken objections that may otherwise be urged against the views she so cogently defends.

After the long series of wars and invasions that racked Europe throughout the Dark Ages, Britain, thanks to her insular position, was able to settle down pretty quickly to a spell of relative peace and political stability under a single monarch. Almost at once a growing demand arose for intelligent and educated men—clerks, lawyers, justices, court bureaucrats and local officers—to assist in the elaborate administrative system created by the Anglo-Norman Kings. The need for talent provoked a search for talent, and inspired new schemes for training it. Reading and writing were still confined almost exclusively to the Church—'the mother of all professions'. The clergy themselves, however, were celibate. Hence they and their successors tended to be recruited from the ablest of the younger sons in any and every social class.

In every other calling both worldly possessions and social functions descended by inheritance—in Britain usually to the first-born. The eldest son of a franklin or yeoman would inherit his father's strip of land and the tools with which to cultivate it. Younger sons set out to seek their fortune; when endowed with both brains and ambition, they often

vii

succeeded. Sir Anthony Wagner (Garter King of Arms) in his book
English Genealogy quotes numerous well-authenticated examples both of
individuals and of families rising and falling from their previous social
rank. It was this increasing mobility, quite as much as the feudal system,
that was responsible for our hierarchy of social classes: and in England
there were evidently nothing like the class-barriers that prevailed on the
continent. Queen Elizabeth I, for example, was descended from a
villein—a rise from the lowest to the highest in only five generations: it
was this, I suspect, that largely accounted for her own exceptional ability.

Under the Plantagenets the monastic schools rapidly expanded.
About the beginning of the thirteenth century the University of Oxford
was founded, with its unique system of colleges—a system peculiar to this
country. Students were drawn from grammar schools, which were
frequently established in association with a particular college, and the
more generous benefactors usually left funds to aid youths of proved
ability who were unable to support themselves. Just after the death of
Edward III, William of Wykeham, his former Chancellor and himself
of humble origin, endowed a 'New College' at Oxford 'for 100 clerks'
and a school at Winchester for '70 pore and needy scholars proficient in
the grammaticals'. This marked the beginning of the British scholarship
system. Under the Tudors and the Stuarts a vast number of endowed
schools were established all over the country by the far-sighted muni-
ficence of wealthy merchants and their guilds.

Throughout these earlier centuries, as the records show, the majority
of the scholars matriculated as '*pleb. fil.*', very few as '*arm. fil.*' (son of a
man entitled to armorial bearings); and even '*gen. fil.*' (of 'gentle' birth)
is rare until the close of the seventeenth century. There was, however, a
sharp reaction. Chamberlayne (1669) attributed the recent 'Sedition
and Rebellion' to the way the county grammar schools had imparted
learning to over-ambitious pupils from the lower classes. 'Never', said
Hobbes, 'was anything so dearly bought'. By the eighteenth century
both public schools and universities had become the preserve of the
privileged upper classes—a situation which many champions of 'social
equality' suppose to have persisted to the present day. Gibbon described
the years he spent at Magdalen as 'the most idle and unprofitable of my
whole life'. And the poet Cowper thought a public school a breeding-
ground for the type of gifted misfit that Dr Pringle has depicted:

> Would you your son should prove a sot or dunce,
> Headstrong, lascivious, or all these at once,
> Train him 'in public' with a mob of boys,
> Childish in mischief only, and in noise.

A revival took place in the middle of the Victorian era. During the first half of the nineteenth-century educational reformers were still greatly influenced by the egalitarian doctrines of the so called 'utilitarians' or 'associationists'—the forerunners of the twentieth-century behaviourists. Arnold of Rugby, it is true, was interested chiefly in the education of the brighter children of the mercantile and middle classes. His success is attested by the fact that three times as many public schools were founded during the next thirty years after his death than in the hundred years before. A few, inspired by the example of the 'dissenting academies', awarded scholarships or exhibitions to 'lads of promise from the deserving poor'. As a result there was an increasing tendency to select pupils on the basis of a written entrance examination. When I won my scholarship to Christ's Hospital, about twenty boys from 'Board Schools' all over the country were annually admitted without fee, provided they passed a rather strenuous 'scholarship examination'.

This policy received a powerful stimulus, and what seemed a scientific sanction, from the work of Sir Francis Galton. His book, *Hereditary Genius*, his 'biological explanation' of the rise and fall of earlier civilisations, his first-hand researches in various schools, and his 'anthropological laboratory where children's mental capacities could be tested and measured', all exercised a profound effect on English educationists towards the turn of the century. To the criticisms of Hobbes and Chamberlayne, re-echoed by many British reformers after the French Revolution and the Chartist movement, he answered that 'sedition and rebellion' are more likely to become rampant when the abler members in the lowlier classes feel themselves frustrated by lack of an appropriate education. To provide an educational ladder up which they might climb would, he maintained, 'ease the recurrent tension among the lower orders and gain fresh talent for the nation'.

Under the London County Council, from 1913 onwards, brief records were kept at the Education Office of the subsequent career of every winner of a junior county scholarship, and special dossiers were compiled of those who gained, or just failed to gain, scholarships to a university. The wide differences between the number of pupils awarded junior scholarships in the poorer boroughs like Bermondsey and Bethnal Green as compared with those in well-to-do boroughs like Hampstead, Wandsworth, and Lewisham was one of the main reasons for appointing an educational psychologist to look into such questions. Surveys carried out with standardised tests revealed that something like a quarter of the children who were endowed with high innate ability were in fact (to adopt a once fashionable phrase) 'underachievers'. It is among these, as Dr Pringle emphasises, that the 'able misfits' are chiefly to be found. As a rule, most of them only come to light during the investigation of other types of problem, such as psychoneurosis or delinquency. Miss Howard, in her studies of maladjustment (*Brit. J. Statist. Psychol.*, V, pp. 39 f. and refs.), found that 'an innate degree of general intelligence *above* the average is apparently a more effective cause of maladjustment than an innate degree *below* the average'; and in our researches on juvenile delinquency we noted an appreciable number of cases in which there was a marked disparity between the child's high capacity and his comparatively low class in school, or between his own sharp wits and the obtuseness of his parents, or again between the cramping poverty from which he suffered and the comparative affluence of the boon companions whom his talents enabled him to cultivate.

In nearly all these cases, it appeared, by far the commonest reason for the misfit was the fact that the child's high ability had never been recognised. The letters and autobiographies of British men of genius abound in testimonies to this effect. Galton himself wrote home from school complaining 'how painful it is to crawl along at the snail's pace of the other fellows in my form': and in his *Memories* he described his school years as 'just a period of stagnation: I learnt nothing, and chafed at the limitations'. Darwin said much the same of his time at Shrewsbury: 'Nothing could have been worse for the development of my mind'. His schoolmasters, we are told, 'thought him a very ordinary boy, rather below the common standard in intellect'. I could quote many similar complaints from my own case-histories. 'At my new grammar school', writes one, 'I was, to begin with, always the first to answer: and my answers were always right. As a result I got sneered at and bullied for being "a swot" and "showing off". So I just lay low.' Others from the very start seem to develop a kind of protective colouring: they conform to the habits and level of the rest of their class: and so their exceptional abilities pass unsuspected. Meanwhile their wits find vent in some other direction—playing the buffoon or becoming ringleaders of an antisocial gang. Educational psychologists are fond of warning us that, 'if a teacher treats an apparent dullard as a genuine dullard, that child will live down to the teacher's expectation'; in the same way, if a teacher treats a brilliant youngster as just an average pupil, that is what he will always remain. For this reason it is of paramount importance to take active measures to detect, at the earliest possible age, those endowed with high but hidden capacities.

Most of the earlier researches on the problem were primarily statistical; their main result was to reveal the unexpected complexity of the processes involved. What is now most urgently needed is a series of intensive case-studies to determine what specific causes are responsible for these warped personalities and their frayed relationships, and then to discover what are the most effective methods of treating and curing them. This is the approach that Dr Pringle has followed. But there is a further reason why her work is specially opportune. During the pre-war period, when most of these earlier surveys were carried out, poverty and other adverse material conditions still played a crucial role. With the advent of the so-called 'Welfare State' and the marked improvement in educational organisation it has become highly desirable that the whole issue should be taken up afresh.

Since Galton and his followers first drew attention to the importance of mental inheritance, there have been further reversals in public opinion. 'We are living', wrote Professor Wiseman (now Director of the National Foundation for Educational Research) a few years ago, 'in a period of egalitarianism, which carries with it a hostility towards the concept of differences in innate ability'. The abolition of the 11-plus examination and the widespread preference for the socalled 'comprehensive' school are largely the result of this change in outlook. In certain respects the recent reorganisation of the education system can justifiably claim to have rectified some of the defects in the older system. Nevertheless, many leading educationists are beginning to argue that a too hasty and too extensive adoption of the comprehensive principle has brought with it many unsuspected dangers. In particular several educational psychologists have independently noted how in their own area the new system has tended to militate against the recognition of gifted pupils in many of the schools and has failed to furnish the special types of curriculum and teaching-methods which such children require. This does not necessarily imply that the system in itself is wrong, but merely that it calls for appropriate modification or for special vigilance. And few will deny that, as Dr Pringle remarks in her opening chapter, 'the study of the gifted child has been sadly neglected'.

The practice of teachers themselves has also changed. During the period between the two wars most of them had, in their student days, been trained by their lecturers in the application and interpretation of standardised tests. A popular device at that time was the calculation of an Achievement Quotient. This, it was believed, enabled one to identify the socalled 'underachievers'. Theoretically, indeed, such a quotient was indefensible; but I doubt whether in practice it led to any serious mistakes. The correct procedure is to take, not the ratio, but the difference between the child's standard measures for intelligence and for attainments, or (what is virtually the same if the tests have been suitably standardised) between his mental age and his educational age (cf. Tables I–IV in this volume, pp. 8–11). However, the violent attacks recently launched by critics of the 'Galtonian capacity theory' (as they like to call it) have made most present-day teachers chary of attempting any such comparisons. The evidence which Dr Pringle has collected will, let us hope, restore the teachers' confidence in the possibility of ascertaining who are gifted and who need help.

Dr Pringle has restricted herself to an intensive study of a small group of representative cases. But, as she points out, this limitation should not lead the reader to underestimate the magnitude of the problem. Data collected about ten years ago, when the 11-plus examination was still favoured by a majority of local authorities, indicated that the number of children of grammar school ability who nevertheless failed to enter a grammar school was somewhere between 5 and 10 per cent. There is nothing to suggest that the percentages have since diminished. Among the more highly gifted children the numbers that fail to receive the education they merit is much larger. In an earlier investigation it was found that, 'of the pupils coming from the non-fee-paying classes nearly half of those possessing the ability to profit by a university education fail to enter a university'. During recent years conditions have undoubtedly improved; but the vast amount of wasted talent still fails to secure recognition.

I for one, therefore, would fully agree with Dr Pringle's criticisms of the 'present situation' and with the various practical proposals that she has put forward in the closing chapters of her book. The first step is obviously to identify those who seem gifted either with high general intelligence or with special abilities or with both. Furthermore, as she rightly contends, the identification should be made, not (as many teachers seem to assume) at the time of the 11-plus examination, but as soon as the child enters school, or better still, if it were only practicable, during the first five years of life. Only thus will it be possible 'to ensure an optimal environment for the development of each child's potentialities'. As regards the special type of curriculum and teaching methods that are needed for the specially gifted, we in this counry have much to learn from the experiments that have been carried out and the practical changes that have been introduced by progressive educationists in the United States. A new mode of approach has been adopted by Dr Bridges at Brentwood College of Education. Small batches of children with exceptionally high I.Q.s, attending primary schools in the neighbourhood, spend a part of each week at the College, where they receive an experimental type of instruction suited, so far as possible, to the individual talents of each. It is too early to pronounce upon the results achieved; but it has already proved a promising line of attack.

Above all, there is a pressing need for further research. Here Dr Pringle has set a valuable example and supplied an instructive model. It is a task in which not only educational psychologists, but teachers themselves can play a useful part. An obvious plan, I venture to suggest, might well be the organisation of a few small-scale investigations in which a matched control-group was intensively studied, side by side with a representative sample of gifted underachievers. This procedure has shed considerable light on such problems as the causes and treatment of delinquency, neuroticism, and educational subnormality; but, strange to say, no comparable study along these lines has been undertaken in the case of intellectually supernormal children. To state that among gifted misfits such and such percentages of cases include broken homes, low cultural backgrounds, unsatisfactory relations with their parents, teachers, or school companions, does not necessarily demonstrate that such factors really act as major causes until we have ascertained the corresponding percentages among gifted children who are not misfits, or indeed among the ordinary school population. What precisely are the specific conditions that should be noted and compared Dr Pringle's inquiry clearly indicates. Her book, therefore, should be read and studied by educational psychologists, by teachers, and, I would add, by all who are interested in the educational welfare of the younger generation.

Introduction: Plan and Purpose of the Book

Human resources

It has almost become a platitude to say that human resources are the most valuable raw material, particularly in a country not otherwise blessed with rich natural resources. High ability, it could be argued, is the most precious asset of all, as it is the mainspring for creating ideas, progress and leadership in all spheres of life. Unused or underused ability is wanton waste. Perhaps worse still, misdirected high ability may potentially be a greater threat to society than the unrealised potential of the less able. Be this as it may, so far little assessment has been attempted of how effectively high ability is being developed and deployed, and how much there remains untapped.

The study of able children, as well as of those with special gifts, has been sadly neglected in this country, though there are now some signs of an awakening interest in their development and needs. Recently the first national study of gifted children in this country was begun by the National Bureau for Co-operation in Child Care. Some experimental schemes have also been introduced in a few areas which aim to provide a specially stimulating or enriched curriculum for able children.

Purpose of the book

Why should able children fail or be misfits at school? The main aim of this book is to provide some answers to these questions and to make some suggestions as to how their number might be reduced. How many able children are misfits in the school population as a whole is unknown at present; and the answer to this question will not be found in this volume.

What will be found is an account of a study—in as non-technical language as possible—of a group of very intelligent children who had behaviour and educational difficulties of various kinds, and who in many cases were not recognised as being particularly able, either by their parents or by their teachers. A background is provided of the more

I

general issues relating to learning, emotion, maladjustment and underachievement. Then some practical suggestions are put forward of how
such difficulties might be prevented, or remedied once they have arisen.

The study on which this book is based was carried out in a teaching
and research unit of a university department. It is primarily a descriptive
account of a group of intelligent children whose difficulties were severe
enough to persuade their teachers or parents to seek psychological
advice. No claim is made that the children are in any way typical of
able but failing pupils. Indeed, it could be argued that they were self-
selected since at least all the parents were willing to take the time and
trouble to bring them along. Moreover, a university clinic inevitably
enjoys greater prestige than local authority psychological services or
child guidance clinics; if for no other reason, because parents can tell
their relatives and neighbours that their child is going to the university!
Furthermore, able but failing children are almost by definition a small
minority group, albeit an important and hitherto much neglected one.

Plan of the book

The conventional and perhaps more logical approach would have been
to start at the beginning, i.e. to discuss the relevant psychological issues
first in general terms; then to present the main findings of the study
together with the statistical results; this to be followed by some case
studies to illustrate the overall results for the whole group; and finally
to consider the practical implications of this and other investigations.
Those who prefer this order of presentation should start by reading
Part 3; then continue with Part 2, to be followed by Part 1; concluding
with the final section, Part 4.

Why, then, has this more tidy, historical approach been discarded
in favour of the layout here adopted, which describes first of all a number
of case histories? The reason for this is that the case histories illustrate
in human, concrete terms, rather than in more generalised, summarised
and impersonal form, the main problems encountered in this study of
able 'misfits'. In this way major issues become more tangible, immediate
and real: they are related to individual children who are brought to
life by recounting their whole history as seen and felt by themselves,
their parents and their teachers. Fictitious names have been used
throughout. Care has been taken to avoid giving details which could
make the identification of children possible; in some instances this has
meant withholding or changing certain facts. This case material is
presented in a non-technical way in the hope that it will be of interest
to all concerned with children but in particular to parents, teachers and
social workers.

Then follows the statistical material, which provides an overall picture of the children and their background. Inevitably this account is more generalised and impersonal, being, as it were, a summarised bird's eye view of the whole group of 103 cases. Both these parts of the book relate specifically to our study.

Next comes a more theoretical section, Part 3. Here the psychology of learning and adjustment is considered in relation to the development and needs of children generally; such issues as the basic psychological needs, the link between learning and emotion, and the meaning and interpretation of symptoms of emotional maladjustment are discussed. This is followed by an account of other research work concerned with able 'misfits', briefly reviewing the main results.

The final part of the book deals with questions of prevention and remedial action. The findings of this and other investigations are related to the practical implications which these have for educational and social policy for able children. Emphasis is given to what parents and teachers could do now, without any allocation of additional resources, if present knowledge and understanding were more readily made available to them and more willingly adopted by them than has been the case hitherto.

The tabulated results have been placed at the end of the book to preserve textual continuity and to minimise the need for statistical analysis on the reader's part.

Acknowledgements

Many people helped, directly and indirectly, to make the writing of this book possible, including my former colleagues in the university who collaborated with me; the teachers who supplied information and co-operated in treatment and the follow-up enquiries; and perhaps, most of all, the children and their parents, who gave us their confidence and accepted the guidance offered. Three people must be mentioned by name: Miss Winifred Watson and Miss J. Worrall, who helped with Chapters 7, 8 and 9; and my husband, W. L. Hooper, who gave me invaluable help with the final editing.

PART 1

Some Case Studies

The origin, methods and findings of the study are described in Part 2, but here—to make all the facts and figures come to life—the stories of a few selected children are related in some detail.

1. The Children and their Stories

It would be a contradiction in terms to speak of a typical exceptional child. Rather, if able children are by definition exceptional, then able misfits are even more so. Selecting from among such a group means no more than choosing some examples to illustrate, in much greater detail than is possible for all 103 children who were studied, the range of circumstances or conditions which are associated with their learning difficulties.

The cases of some sixteen children, twelve boys and four girls, are presented under four broad headings, each characterising what appeared to be the most salient unfavourable feature in the child's background: too high parental expectations; too low parental expectations; emotional stress in the home; and the effect of physical handicap. Of course, these features are by no means mutually exclusive.

The test results and the outstanding personality traits of each child, as well as his parents' attitude towards him, are shown in summary form (Tables 1 to 4). An identical pattern of presentation has been adopted for each case. First, the child's name (always, of course, fictitious), age, mental age, intelligence quotient and attainment ages are given and the source of referral, together with the main reasons for it, are stated. Then the child's reaction towards and behaviour during the psychological interview are described, followed by the school's view of him. Information about the family and parental attitudes, obtained by the psychiatric social worker, follows. Finally the recommendations made in each case and subsequent developments are summarised and a prognosis is given.

The amount of detail with which each case is described varies from child to child, according to the complexity of the circumstances. But even the longest of the case histories is a highly condensed summary of all the information which was available and an even smaller fraction—merely a bird's eye view—of the child's actual life and all that shaped it.

7

Table 1. Too high parental expectations (N = 6)

Name	Age	Mental age	I.Q.	Reading age	Spelling age	Arithmetic age	No. of siblings	Outstanding personality traits	Father's job	Mother's job	Parental attitude to child
1. IAN	6–11	9–6	140	7–1	5–6	6–9	2s	Timid, dreamy, solitary, dislikes school, bedwetter and stammers	Clergyman	Ex-nurse	High standards and expectations, disappointed at lack of drive and over-imaginativeness
2. JONATHAN	8–6	11–4	132	7–6	6–6	8–4	1b	Good at games and at art, popular, 'scatter-brained'	Headmaster	Nursery school teacher	Ambitious, impatient and driving; both quite strict
3. SIMON	11–9	18–0	143	13–11	12–11	16–0	None	Self-sufficient, detached, shows little affection, more interested in hobbies than school work	University teacher	Ex-secretary	Father strict and rejecting; mother weak, inconsistent and baffled
4. JOHN	9–0	13–6	146	10–7	9–2	8–4	1s	Aggressive, always in trouble and a ring leader, lazy, bully	Businessman	Ex-shop assistant	Father over-ambitious, strict and indulgent; mother weak, ineffective
5. JIMMY	13–4	17–10	129	13–6	12–11	11–2	1s	Gentle, slow, very dependent on younger sister	Medical research worker	Medical research worker	Both so taken up by their careers little time for the children
6. JEAN (sister of Jimmy (5))	9–3	12–6	132	10–6	9–0	8–8	1b	Competent but rather bossy, cannot be driven, works when interested	as above	as above	Ambitious educationally

Table 2. Too low parental expectations (N = 4)

Name	Age	Mental age	I.Q.	Reading age	Spelling age	Arithmetic age	No. of siblings	Outstanding personality traits	Father's job	Mother's job	Parental attitude to child
7. SHEILA (sister of John (4))	10–1	14–0	134	13–8	12–6	9–6	1b	Lacking in confidence, timid, solitary	Businessman	Ex-shop assistant	Lacking in interest and support, rejected
8. BEN	11–1	16–1	138	12–6	10–5	9–6	1s	Poised, confident, sophisticated	Industrialist	Starlet	Treated like a pet, ignored most of the time
9. CHARLES	11–0	17–7	150	16++	15++	16–10	None	Confident, quick-witted, charming, imaginative	Civil servant (clerical grade)	Ex-typist	Indulgent, doting gently ineffectual
10. GILLIAN	9–10	12–0	127	9–9	7–2	8–2	1s	Fearful, inhibited and dependent	Gas Board inspector	Ex-shop assistant	Over-protective and over-anxious, doting

Table 3. Emotional stress in the home (N = 3)

Name	Age	Mental age	I.Q.	Reading age	Spelling age	Arithmetic age	No. of siblings	Outstanding personality traits	Father's job	Mother's job	Parental attitude to child
11. ALBERT	7–7	10–6	139	5–8	5–3	below norms	3s	Withdrawn, anxious, solitary, tense	Unskilled labourer	Cleaner	Concerned but ineffectual
12. PAUL	13–5	21–10	156	all above the norms			1b	Detached, dreamy, solitary, arrogant, sensitive	Café owner	Ex-waitress	Father over-demanding; mother over-indulgent and inconsistent
13. BETTY	6–6	9–6	149	10–0	8–0	6–0	none	Self-willed, aggressive, domineering, destructive	Research chemist	Maths teacher	Father indulgent, gentle; mother strict, obsessional, punitive, over-possessive

Table 4. The effect of physical handicap (N = 3)

Name	Age	Mental age	I.Q.	Reading age	Spelling age	Arithmetic age	No. of siblings	Outstanding personality traits	Father's job	Mother's job	Parental attitude to child
14. TOBY	9–9	13–4	133	7–2	6–8	9–6	1s	Poised, sense of humour, affectionate	Engineer	Ex-secretary	Affectionate, united, sensible discipline and realistic expectations
15. MARTIN	5–11	11–1	175	10–0	9–2	7–1	2s	Cheerful, determined, lively, outgoing	Accountant	Teacher	Affectionate, united, sensible discipline
16. JACK	10–9	16–2	142	13–8	11–6	12–4	2s 2b	Lively, imaginative, warm-hearted, cheerful	Labourer	Cleaner	Warm-hearted, easy-going, and somewhat indulgent; over-anxious since accident

2. Too High Parental Expectations

The six children described in this chapter all have parents whose educational expectations are high. These are not matched, however, either by the giving of affectionate support or by the necessary cultural stimulation. Thus the children suffer from some emotional neglect or even rejection; and their high intellectual abilities are not being fostered, let alone stretched, by parental interest and participation in their activities. Nor have they been fortunate in meeting teachers who have awakened their curiosity. In fact, all except one child were thought by their schools to be of average ability only. On grounds of educational attainment only, such an opinion was justified in every case except Simon's (p. 24), since scholastic achievement was either below or approximately at the child's actual age rather than at the level of his mental age. (In the descriptions which follow equivalent ages are abbreviated as: M.A., mental age; R.A., reading age; S.A., spelling age; A.A., arithmetic age.)

1. **Ian,** aged 6 yr, 11 mth: M.A. 9 yr, 6 mth; I.Q. 140; R.A. 7 yr, 1 mth; S.A. 5 yr, 6 mth; A.A. 6 yr, 9 mth.

   Referred by a paediatrician because of his stammer and backwardness in spelling.

THE CHILD
A small, pale boy, who during the early part of the interview was patently ill at ease. From time to time he furtively glanced at me but avoided meeting my eyes. He sat on the edge of the chair, answered questions in monosyllables wherever possible and when unable or unwilling to make a reply, chewed his collar. There was a pronounced stammer to begin with but as he became more confident and relaxed, his speech improved quite considerably. Then he began to use longer and more difficult words, showing a good vocabulary and excellent reasoning powers.

Praise for his performance seemed to take him aback at first; gradually he became really absorbed in what he was asked to do, showing good powers of concentration and perseverance. However, he remained very self-critical and ready to denigrate the results of his work. His two older sisters were evidently held up to him as examples: on several occasions he volunteered his conviction that they would be able to cope much better with a particular task than he could.

When it came to the educational tests, he apologised for being very slow and, 'I am not very accurate, either, my daddy always says.' When he was reassured that he was not doing badly and that, anyhow, what counted most was how hard he tried, he protested: 'Making an effort is just not enough, it is the standard of your actual work which counts.' Clearly, there was father's voice again. Similarly, when he reached the limit of his ability on the arithmetic test and was told 'after all, you are still in the infants school, so you can't be expected to do these hard sums', he replied 'You must not make excuses for me, this is what I always do myself. My daddy says I don't put my mind to it 'cause I'm an idle dreamer.'

During a break in the psychological interview, he had a go on some climbing apparatus and tried his skill with a punch ball. In both activities he was rather timid and clumsy. His self-critical attitude was again much in evidence. However, while shown how he might cope better, he seemed to enjoy the physical contact and then continued to keep close to me, often holding my hand. His need for reassurance and affection was also clearly revealed on the personality tests he was given; both parents were seen as stern, demanding and emotionally remote. There was much evidence of his having a lively imagination and a vivid turn of phrase. Fears of failure and anxiety about disapproval dominated his stories, yet he also created imaginary companions who brought magical release from failure and exciting discoveries in a make-believe world.

By the end of the morning, Ian talked very freely about home and school. The hurly-burly of the infant school, especially in the playground, rather frightened him, probably partly because of his small size. He had no friends and constantly worried about his stammer: 'You see, I never know whether I shall be able to get it out.' Having to read aloud in class was torture yet he reasonably commented: 'We all have to do it and I suppose teacher must not make an exception.' At home, his greatest joy were some goldfish and a canary, even though they were apparently substitutes for having a dog, for which he longed passionately but without hope. There seemed to be little contact between him and his sisters, who were considerably older and close to each other in age and interests.

From the level of Ian's conversation and reasoning, as well as from the results of the intelligence tests, there was no doubt about his good ability. His educational attainments, however, were only just average for his age, while his physical co-ordination was somewhat below average. Emotionally he appeared to be rather immature, lacking in confidence and timid in making relationships; yet he had remained very ready to respond to encouragement, praise and affection. So much so that before leaving he confided that he would prefer coming to our clinic every day instead of going to school.

SCHOOL

His class teacher described Ian as a timid, dreamy and solitary boy who rarely volunteered any information during 'news time' when most children vied with one another for a hearing. While his attainments were about average for his age he appeared less able than that because of his slowness. When told about his high intellectual ability the teacher was frankly sceptical, though conceded that Ian's stammer might make one underestimate his oral work. He was thought to be far less able than his two sisters who had been to the same school. The parents were said to be most interested in his progress and the home was described as being excellent.

FAMILY CIRCUMSTANCES

The father was a clergyman and his wife an ex-nurse, who on marriage gave up work. For financial reasons the parents delayed starting a family and then two girls were born within eighteen months of each other. During the early years of their married life, the family had moved about a good deal. Just before Ian's birth, the father was appointed lecturer in divinity and chaplain to a teacher training college, and since then they had settled down in the small country town in which they were still living. The father's time was taken up with his work and he saw little of his son. In any case, he was a rather austere, detached and extremely serious-minded man. He admitted to having little interest in small children and to not knowing how to talk to them; he had only begun to enjoy his daughters when they were in their teens. While he had hoped for easier contact with his son, this hope had proved illusory, partly 'because he always seemed afraid of me'.

The mother also did not give the impression of being a particularly warm, maternal woman. It may well be that the father's and her own disappointment in Ian had led to her apparently detached, critical and almost rejecting attitude towards the boy. The home was well run and beautifully, almost too neatly, kept. Though the mother did a good deal of voluntary work, she was always at home when Ian returned from school. In fact, in all the basic ways, both parents were excellent in providing consistent and conscientious care. What seemed lacking was warmth, enjoyment, a sharing of interests and a desire to stimulate Ian's imagination and curiosity.

PARENTAL ATTITUDES

Both parents very much wanted to have a boy, but after trying for some seven years had given up hope. Then when his mother was forty-five and the father fifty years old, Ian was born; the two girls were by that time fifteen and sixteen and a half years of age. Thus for practical purposes he was an only child with rather elderly parents.

To what extent their age contributed to the rigidity of their outlook is difficult to judge. There were some indications that both parents had always had high, as well as rather conventional, standards. Possibly, too, their hopes for Ian had been so excessive as to make disappointment almost inevitable. His father wanted him to be both a scholar and an athlete, since his own father had been the latter and he thought of himself as the former; his own ambition and hope was still to become a university teacher. The mother had found her daughters easy to bring up and they had done reasonably well in school without particularly distinguishing themselves. Both intended to train as teachers and the parents were content with their choice of career. One gained the impression of cheerful, biddable girls, who had possibly been closer to each other than to their parents.

Ian, on the other hand, had caused his parents concern right from the beginning. He was a rather puny baby; though very forward in talking, especially for a boy, he was slow in walking and in becoming dry, particularly at night; he tended to be 'oversensitive and over-imaginative' which in the father's eyes were undesirable traits in a boy. At the age of four he developed a stammer. It coincided with a number of events, some, if not all, of which may have been associated with it. Both his sisters left home to live in a shared flat; Ian began attending a nursery school in the hope that it would help him overcome his timidity and teach him to mix with other children; his mother had to go into hospital for an operation and an aunt, whom he did not know well, came to look after him. Shortly after this, his father had also to be away from home, to be with his own mother who was dying.

Ian had been taken the rounds of specialists and hospitals because of his continued nocturnal bedwetting and stammer. The former complaint had failed to respond to treatment and the latter, the parents had been assured, he would 'outgrow' in time. Meanwhile he was a disappointment to them all round: three years of schooling had not modified his timidity but, if anything, made it worse; his vivid imagination coupled with his dreamy slowness was a constant source of irritation to both parents; while his bedwetting and stammer caused them to feel ashamed 'as if it were our fault'. Worst of all, his slow educational progress convinced them that he was of barely average intelligence.

This conclusion had not been accepted lightly by either parent. To begin with the father tried to teach Ian to read in an attempt to 'put him ahead of the other children'. When this led to arguments between the parents as to the most suitable methods, both for teaching and for punishing the boy when he did not concentrate, and to Ian's hiding himself to escape these reading lessons, the father eventually engaged a private coach. Though she met with more success (in addition to tears and nightmares) Ian had not become the fluent reader his father wished him to be. The fact that being read to by his mother was still regarded by the boy as being a very special treat, was seen by his father as another sign of his babyishness and lack of intelligence.

SUMMARY AND RECOMMENDATIONS

All the evidence suggested that Ian was an able but very discouraged and educationally underfunctioning boy. Parental, and particularly paternal, expectations were ill-suited to this sensitive, imaginative, rather timid child. While he needed affectionate encouragement and wide-ranging intellectual stimulation, he was in fact left largely to his own resources. Nor did school provide him with the haven, or at least refuge, which could have lowered the tension under which he was living and, better still, enabled him to make use of and thus derive pleasure from his considerable intellectual abilities. Little wonder that he reacted to the weight of pressures by becoming even more timid, withdrawn and dreamy and that he developed psychosomatic stress symptoms (stammer and bedwetting). The fact that he could respond relatively quickly to a more encouraging atmosphere, however, suggested that he might be helped by play therapy and remedial treatment. It was also suggested that fairly intensive case work should be attempted with both parents, though the prognosis for modifying their attitudes did not appear too favourable.

SUBSEQUENT DEVELOPMENTS

For a period of eighteen months Ian attended once a week for a two-hour session. During this time his mother had regular interviews with a psychiatric social worker, while the father came at less frequent intervals. As feared, both parents proved to be rather inflexible, dogmatic and somewhat self-righteous in their attitudes. Though pleased when told about the boy's very good intellectual potential, this knowledge made them for a time even more impatient with his shortcomings. Gradually they were helped to attain some measure of insight into their own feelings and reactions; as well as some understanding of the influence these exerted on Ian's behaviour and adjustment.

The boy himself blossomed under the individual attention he was being given by a sympathetic adult ready to listen. He decided to keep a diary of events, both real and imaginary, which took place during his weekly sessions. To begin with he dictated his account, but gradually agreed to write some parts himself, given, of course, all necessary help with spelling. Eventually he accepted the suggestion to make brief entries at home during the intervening days. His parents had to be dissuaded from wanting to inspect these in order to correct 'inaccuracies of fact, grammar or spelling'.

Ian's weekly sessions resembled nothing so much as a brook which had been dammed up—he chattered incessantly, often growing extremely excited and forceful. The last twenty minutes or so were always used for reading to him, not only to stimulate a real interest in what books could offer but also to calm him down before returning to his mother. He treasured this period during which he would sit very close and at times, in fact, on my lap. Eventually he asked to be allowed to take a book home to finish reading it by himself. During the first term he showed little interest in other children, retreating into his shell if he could not avoid a confrontation (which had been planned in the hope of encouraging his social development). Gradually he became willing to take part in some group activities but only for brief periods.

Despite the school's scepticism regarding Ian's good ability, they were willing to co-operate with us, especially as his timidity and non-participation in most group activities had caused concern. As he grew less monosyllabic, so flashes of insight and unexpectedly mature reasoning began to show themselves. There were also other indications of a good mind so that his teachers felt challenged by his unrealised potential. In turn, their increasing interest and encouragement had beneficial effects on his confidence and thus performance.

At the end of eighteen months, the situation was sufficiently improved for Ian's parents to worry that he was missing a morning's schooling. He himself was extremely anxious to continue coming, but it was felt unwise to let him do so in the face of growing parental resistance. Moreoever, it had been realised from the beginning that one could not

2

expect a radical change in their attitude, though they had certainly modified their handling of the boy. So his visits were put first on a fortnightly and then on a monthly basis prior to complete termination.

PROGNOSIS

What of his future prospects? A mildly optimistic prognosis seems justified: Ian is likely to remain a sensitive, imaginative and rather vulnerable boy, whose early experience of 'failure' will have heightened his susceptibility to retreat from challenge and difficulty. On the positive side, he has been helped to develop some interests, has learned to read fluently, which has opened up a whole new world to him, and has gained some belief in his own abilities, which are also receiving greater recognition at home and at school. The bedwetting has become infrequent and the stammer is in evidence only at times of stress.

Finally, did Ian's good intellectual ability play a significant part in his difficulties? No clearcut answer is possible. On the one hand, it may have made him more sensitive to parental disappointment; but it also made it easier to give him some insight into his own difficulties and to make it possible for him to gain confidence, because his abilities quickly enabled him to make use of appropriate opportunities both at home and at school. Moreover, being able to tell parents and teachers after a psychological examination that the child they are concerned about is of very good intelligence undoubtedly has a positive effect, however unpalatable the rest of the diagnosis and prognosis may be. On the other hand, excessively high parental expectations are not confined to intellectually able children; nor is there evidence that in this instance inappropriate child-rearing methods were due to, or closely associated with, the boy's good ability.

2. Jonathan, aged 8 yr, 6 mth: M.A. 11 yr, 4 mth; I.Q. 132; R.A. 7 yr, 6 mth; S.A. 6 yr, 6 mth; A.A. 8 yr, 4 mth.

Referred by the school because of lack of concentration, disruptive behaviour and backwardness in English subjects.

THE CHILD

A well-built, attractive boy with a ready smile and great charm of manner. Though lively and talkative, his attention wandered a good deal: partly because he wanted to pursue his own ideas and associations rather than be confined to replying to questions; and partly because difficult problems, to which he could not quickly find a solution, seemed to irritate him. When unable to produce an answer, he proceeded to quiz me on the self-same question, thus neatly turning the tables. When this proved unacceptable, he would volunteer some information on a different topic, saying; 'Let me tell you about something else instead.' In this way it soon became evident that he seemed to have a vast store of information of a rather superficial and oddly assorted kind. He had been made aware of this by his father whom he quoted as saying to him: 'You have a magpie mind, which merely collects facts.' Being a good mimic seemed to be among Jonathan's gifts, since he produced not only the appropriate voice but also a suitable facial expression. Then he quickly drew a bird, a dustbin and a grasshopper, commenting; 'All these portray my mind: my class teacher says it's like a dustbin, stuffed full of useless rubbish, and the vicar who takes R.I. says it's like a grasshopper.' This comment was again accompanied by an appropriate change in voice, from falsetto for his woman teacher to a ponderous bass for the vicar.

There was little doubt about his dislike of school, which he expressed in most forceful terms. The fact that his father was also his headmaster, seemed to him the last straw. His favourite subjects were art and games, though he added that 'speed rather than technique is my strength', quoting again an adult's observation on his weakness. However, these strictures seemed to afford him vast amusement rather than regret or resentment. When asked to do some educational tests, he became affronted, saying, 'Why waste time on these? You can see my school reports if you want to know how bad I am. I thought I was here to discuss my future schooling with you.' Eventually he consented to do them on the understanding that they would be 'different from the stuff I have to do in school'. The results showed that, except for arithmetic, his attainments were not even up to his chronological, let alone his mental age level.

Throughout the interview Jonathan showed considerable physical restlessness as well as insatiable curiosity. While an amusing and lively companion, it was easy to see that in a large class he would be a sore trial to any teacher: his irrepressible sense of fun, restless energy, lack of persistence and dislike of facing difficulties would tend to be disruptive of discipline.

SCHOOL

The class teacher considered that Jonathan was correctly placed in a B stream even though he was not quite up to the standard of the majority. When told of his good ability, she commented, 'He shows some superficial brightness because he is such a mimic and can't stop clowning. But he is scatterbrained, inattentive and a nuisance.' Though his art work showed promise, 'he is too slapdash about it'. He was said to be good at games and very popular among his peers. 'A cheerful, happy-go-lucky boy, lacking in application' was the school's summary of his personality.

FAMILY CIRCUMSTANCES

The father, a first generation graduate, was a slightly pompous man, very aware of his position as the youngest headmaster in the town. Though he realised that 'in theory it might be difficult, being a pupil in a school of which your father is the headmaster', he felt certain that Jonathan was too easy-going and insensitive a child to be affected by it. Moreover, he had made quite certain that the boy was treated no differently from anyone else; as an example the father cited his suggesting to the class teacher that the boy should be put forward for a psychological examination because of his lack of application and disruptive behaviour. It had not crossed his mind that one of the reasons for Jonathan's playing the clown and being a nuisance in school was to ensure that no one could suspect him of being 'teacher's pet' on account of his father's position.

Jonathan's brother, three years his junior, seemed to be a more amenable child. The father felt closer to him, 'partly because he takes after me and partly because I've spent more time with him, while I was too busy establishing myself during Jonathan's early years'. Clearly he was pinning all his ambitions on to the younger boy and hiding his disappointment in his older son by saying: 'He'll never amount to much scholastically but his amusing ways will smooth his paths. But he must learn to concentrate and accept discipline.'

The mother, a nursery school teacher, refused to be overawed by father or to take life as seriously as he did. She saw much of herself in Jonathan, shared his sense of humour and recognized that he learned quickly when his interest was aroused. While a little disappointed that his school work was so erratic, she felt there was plenty of time for him to show the at least good average ability which she was convinced was there. She was equally convinced that being in his father's school made things more difficult for him; however, since the only alternatives were a rather long journey or a private school, she reluctantly agreed with her husband that 'it would not do to send our children there, when I am head of a state primary school'.

PARENTAL ATTITUDES

While trying consciously not to be the 'heavy-handed authoritarian', the father had the drive, self-discipline and ambitions of the self-made man who had triumphed over his own limited social and cultural background. He believed that his strict upbringing had contributed to his success and was constantly irritated by Jonathan's lighthearted flippancy. 'Punishment just bounces off him; you can't get through,' was the father's complaint; his reaction to it was greater strictness together with a refusal 'to be amused,' even when Jonathan was being really witty in his imitations of relatives and friends.

By inclination, the mother would have liked to be more tolerant and appreciative of the boy's good points. Loyalty to her husband and a feeling that consistent discipline was probably preferable to parents pulling in different directions, led her to adopt his standards and attitudes, especially once Jonathan started going to school. Despite this overt bowing to her husband's judgment she could not bring herself to suppress entirely her delight in the boy's sense of fun, his lively curiosity and his passion for facts 'even if they were useless'. She blamed herself for having sent him to nursery school 'for the wrong reasons', her husband's insistence that she was spoiling him and Jonathan's tendency to be jealous of his younger brother and be rough with him. She thought he had learned to play the clown as a means of gaining the individual attention he needed and which she could have provided herself much more effectively than could a teacher busy with a whole group of children.

Having also been considered a scatterbrained child, the mother still remembered the feeling of helplessness in the face of adult criticism; yet the condemnation of this trait had been well inculcated in her. So she was torn between disapproval, understanding and a desire to protect him from the misery this characteristic had caused her at home and at school. Yet it made her feel guilty that Jonathan seemed to be aware of her tolerant sympathy. Without realising it, her mixed feelings about herself, her husband and Jonathan produced a constant undertone of inconsistent parental attitudes, cloaked by a superficially united front.

SUMMARY AND RECOMMENDATIONS

Temperamentally rather like his mother, Jonathan had found refuge from paternal pressure in opting out of scholastic competition and gaining satisfaction from playing the clown. Though his art work was said to show promise, it, too, was marred by his happy-go-lucky, impetuous approach. He collected facts, partly because they intrigued him as well as other people, and partly because 'the horror, which is my brother, can't get at them as he does at all my other things'. His good ability had remained unrecognised, both at home and at school, since it was as yet unchannelled and overshadowed by his nuisance value to adults in authority. Children responded to his sense of fun, his inventiveness in games and his athletic abilities; also they secretly admired his easy-going acceptance of reproof and punishment.

It was felt that as a first step, both Jonathan and his brother would benefit from not attending their father's primary school (the younger brother showed every sign of being a 'model' child). Even though transfer to another primary school meant a much longer journey, as well as obtaining special permission from the Education Department because of zoning restrictions, this possibility seemed worth exploring. Not only would it give the boy another start but also the school in question was unstreamed; Jonathan was likely to respond better to a non-competitive atmosphere in which he could work at his own pace. Furthermore, the teacher in whose class he would be placed was known for his interest in children who had special difficulties. Having done a lot for dull and maladjusted youngsters, he felt challenged by an able, underfunctioning pupil and the added complication of his being the son of teachers.

Second, the parents were offered a series of interviews to discuss how each of them might help Jonathan to make more positive use of his good potential and his personal qualities.

Third, they were assured that if there was no appreciable acceleration in the boy's scholastic progress after he had been in his new school for a year, he would be accepted for remedial treatment in our department.

SUBSEQUENT DEVELOPMENTS

Jonathan settled well in his new school. Though there was no dramatic improvement in his educational attainment, he no longer regarded all activities, other than games and art, as a waste of time to be endured as best he could. The opportunity to work on his own, move around the classroom and follow through a particular interest seemed to have a beneficial effect, compared with the previous traditional teaching approach, which had increased his restlessness. His new teacher appreciated his gift of mimicry and was amused by his clowning, regarding neither as a challenge to his authority. And he harnessed Jonathan's passion for facts by prevailing upon him to produce a weekly 'broadsheet of events', as well illustrated and as well documented as he could make it, by using encyclopaedias and other reference books; for this purpose reading became an essential tool, to the mastery of which Jonathan now became willing to devote considerable persistence.

At the end of the term, he was encouraged to combine his broadsheets into an alphabetically arranged 'book', which he was taught how to bind. It was a really creditable effort which called out some grudging admiration even from his father.

The interviews with his parents also met with a measure of success. The father came to see that temperamentally the boy was much more like his mother; that the personal qualities which had stood him in such good stead, were not necessarily essential to his son's growing into a successful or fulfilled adult; that it would help both the relationship between the parents, and between them and Jonathan, if they openly recognised their rather different attitudes to life and, hence, to the personalities of their two rather different sons; and that such recognition need not lead to inconsistent handling or to increased uncertainty. Children invariably sensed differences and conflicts, and suffered much more when these were never brought out into the open. Learning that differences of opinion and of attitudes did not imply a lack of affection was part of growing up and an invaluable lesson, if learnt within the relative security of family life.

Both parents were helped to see that they had treated the brothers as if they were practically of the same age; and that Jonathan needed to be given much more of his father's time. By doing things together and by pursuing an interest in greater depth than he was capable of doing on his own, Jonathan might be helped to 'learn to concentrate' much more effectively than by merely being told to do so. Ways were suggested of harnessing his sense of humour and his artistic abilities to more specifically educational activities, both at home and at school.

PROGNOSIS

Provided the father can allow Jonathan to develop and follow his artistic and athletic abilities without making him feel that such talents are merely second-best pursuits, the outlook should be reasonably hopeful. Receiving more open and less guilt-ridden recognition from his mother, together with the recently won approval of his teacher, had already improved matters for the time being; the removal from his father's school had also helped to reduce the boy's need to rebel.

The type of secondary education best suited to Jonathan's gifts and interests was likely to be a disturbing issue to the father, especially if the boy should fail to reach a high enough level of educational attainment to pass the examination for selective secondary schooling.

This in fact happened. Jonathan continued to make good educational progress and thus did not require remedial help. On the other hand entry to grammar schools was highly competitive in the town where the family lived and he just missed gaining a place. Though he eventually trained as an art teacher and grew into a delightfully amusing young man of great charm and vitality, his father could never rid himself of the feeling that such gaiety was a sign of a basic irresponsibility; on his part

Jonathan tolerantly, though with a touch of condescension, referred to
'the worthy, if pompous, earnestness of the old man'.

3. Simon, aged 11 yr, 9 mth; M.A. 18 yr; I.Q. 143; R.A. 13 yr, 11 mth;
S.A. 12 yr, 11 mth; A.A. 16 yr.

Referred by the school for advice on his future schooling.

THE CHILD

A tall, thin boy who seemed unusually self-contained for his age. While
he co-operated well enough during the interview, success and praise
made relatively little difference to his effort and he knew when a problem
was beyond him. He made few spontaneous comments and showed a
curiously detached, almost aloof attitude. Subsequently it emerged that
this characterised his behaviour both at home and at school.

According to his own judgment he was 'rather a trial to my teacher
because I am bored most of the time and don't try'. Though he read
well, he rarely did so for pleasure but mainly for information which he
needed to follow his hobby of model-making and chemical experiments.
'At present I do neither at school but I am told there will at least be
some science when I go to a new school in the autumn.'

Even when talking about his hobbies he grew only marginally more
enthusiastic and would soon have dried up, had he not been encouraged
to describe them at greater length. He had no 'real friends' nor did he
seem to feel the lack of them: 'They rather get in your way when you
want to press on with an experiment.'

SCHOOL

Having just failed to gain entry into a grammar school, the parents
proposed to send Simon to a private school, since for social reasons they
rejected both secondary modern and comprehensive schools. The
present headmaster felt concerned, since in his view the boy's good
ability was unlikely to receive the necessary stimulation in the establishment of the parents' choice; also, he wondered why Simon should
have remained so unresponsive a pupil. Though always in an A class
and never 'any trouble', he rarely cared enough to make an effort; even
in mathematics, his favourite subject, he did the minimum. The headmaster now regretted not having insisted on psychological advice earlier,
but when he had suggested it the father would not hear of it.

FAMILY CIRCUMSTANCES

The father, a professor of anthropology, had rather late in life married
his much younger secretary. To begin with she had accompanied him

on his field trips abroad but her enthusiasm had waned quickly. Since Simon's birth she no longer went with her husband but resented the long periods she was left by herself. Not being a particularly maternal woman, she was relieved when told she was unlikely to have more children; for the same reason she rejected the idea of adopting a child which her husband had thought would be company for Simon. He had himself been an only child and had always blamed this for his inability to make friendships in later life.

PARENTAL ATTITUDES

The relationship between father and son remained a distant one, partly because he was away a good deal and partly because he considered young children tediously boring. He had hoped that his love of games would later on become a shared interest, but to his disappointment Simon proved to be physically timid and without any aptitude in this direction. Neither persuasion nor shock tactics were of any avail; in fact, having been thrown into a swimming pool by his father, the boy could not go near water without becoming sick. Otherwise, Simon conformed fairly readily to the strict discipline on which his father insisted but this, too, displeased the father as 'showing a lack of spunk'.

The mother had become a very dissatisfied woman. Once the glamour of marrying her boss and a don, had worn off, she was bored and lonely since she had found university wives to be standoffish and had felt obliged to discontinue her friendships with her previous office friends. Her disappointment in having a boy rather than a girl was made worse by his being a 'very uncuddly baby'. Eventually she acquired two toy poodles on which she lavished a great deal of time and affection. Her handling of Simon was a mixture of indulgence, inconsistency and baffled defeat: 'He obeys his father instantly but I can never be sure how he'll behave; often he is as good as gold and you'd hardly know he is in the house; then he'll suddenly go all stubborn and there is nothing I can do about it.'

To keep him occupied, Simon had always been showered with toys, but rarely had either parent played with him. When he developed his interest in model-making and in chemical experiments, the garden shed was fitted up with a work bench and from then on 'he would potter about happily for hours'.

The father's hope for an intellectual son whose guide and mentor he could become, had been dashed by what he called Simon's 'practical, largely manipulative interests.' These meant nothing to the father, a highly articulate, literate man, to whom a lack of verbal skills was a sure sign of limited intellectual ability. To the mother, Simon's lack of academic success meant that she felt again inferior in comparison with the many 'university wives' who could boast one or more outstandingly able children. On the other hand, both parents spoke approvingly of Simon's self-sufficient, detached attitude and his capacity to keep himself amused. His lack of affection was ascribed to their 'not being a demonstrative family'.

SUMMARY AND RECOMMENDATIONS

Though home for Simon was an emotionally barren and intellectually unstimulating place, the likelihood of bringing about any real change within a reasonable time seemed remote: the father's age (58) and frequent absence from home, and the mother's relative lack of intelligence and maternal warmth, made modifying their attitudes and giving them some insight into the boy's needs a task hardly worth attempting.

Instead, the question of boarding school was explored and when Simon seemed quite keen on the idea, it was put to the parents. The school which was suggested catered primarily for normal children but was willing to accept a few who needed special help. It was co-educational, relatively small and organised along family lines, with married couples being responsible for groups of children. Though the atmosphere was not unduly competitive, the results achieved in art and science were quite outstanding.

After some initial hesitation—largely on grounds of finance—the parents took Simon to see the school and eventually agreed to his going there.

SUBSEQUENT DEVELOPMENT

Simon's progress was followed for a period of seven years. Rather unexpectedly he enjoyed coming to pay a visit to our department during each of the school holidays, though gradually this tailed off to become a yearly call. The school sent reports regularly which showed that though he remained somewhat of a 'lone wolf', Simon improved considerably over the years. He became very attached to his science master and to the headmaster's wife, and passed through a somewhat stormy period of being overdemanding and resentfully jealous of other pupils. During these periods of emotional crises his school work deteriorated, but during calmer times he made big strides forward. He became a good chess player, reasonably proficient at cricket and passionately fond of music.

While chess and cricket became something of a bond between father and son, the gulf between him and his mother grew steadily wider. Though he did well enough to have stood a good chance of getting into a university, Simon wanted to be economically independent at the earliest opportunity: his father was near retirement and had anyhow never let him forget that the need to pay fees had in the first place been due to his not exerting himself enough to win a free place at a grammar school. So he accepted a trainee post in the research department of a large industrial firm.

PROGNOSIS

Reasonably good, though it looks doubtful whether he will ever use to the full his good intellectual abilities. One also wonders what kind of husband and father he will eventually make if he does not find some equilibrium between the detached self-sufficiency which he had acquired at an early age, and the jealous, overdemanding possessiveness which he developed during adolescence.

4. **John,** aged 9 yr; M.A. 13 yr, 6 mth; I.Q. 146; R.A. 10 yr, 7 mth; S.A. 9 yr, 2 mth; A.A. 8 yr, 4 mth.

Referred by the school because of constant bullying and 'not trying despite reasonable ability'.

THE CHILD

A sturdy boy, big for his age, confident and rather self-assertive. He enjoyed the challenge of the new situation but his interest was not sustained and he needed a good deal of encouragement to persevere. On the way to the interviewing room he had noticed a punch-ball and some climbing ropes, which he was anxious to try out. The promise that he could do so provided he did some work first had to be used as a bribe to get him through the educational tests, which he particularly disliked. Overall, his attainments were at best average for his age but his actual school performance was likely to be even worse since he was at logger-heads with his teachers.

Physical activities evidently called out all his energies and he showed himself to be agile, well co-ordinated and fearless.

SCHOOL

Described as a ringleader and bully, he had been a trial to his teachers from the beginning. He did a minimum of work to get by, was impatient and careless, and reacted to correction with surly defiance. Matters had come to a head when he had knocked out another boy, though it was partly bad luck rather than design that he fell, hitting his head on a stake. However, the headmaster had used this opportunity to give the father the choice of expulsion or referral, which he had resisted before, taunting the head with inability to cope with a mere boy. It was John's constant aggressiveness as much as his inadequate scholastic performance which had led the school to take this step.

FAMILY CIRCUMSTANCES
The father had worked his way up from a garage hand to owning a flourishing garage himself; his wife had been a shop assistant and after her marriage had helped to build up the business, making various child-minding arrangements for John and his sister. An aggressive, forceful and rather arrogant man, her husband had an ambivalent attitude towards education: he regretted having had to leave school early to earn his living, '"cause I was as bright if not brighter than the next lad', yet he despised 'them la-di-da, cissy intellectuals'. Nothing was too good for his son who, he was convinced, had inherited his own ability, toughness and determination to prove himself. It was his ambition that John should become a famous scientist or explorer, and to this end he would give him the best education which money could buy. That his garage prevented him spending much time with the boy was a matter for regret but 'I haven't much to teach him myself when I can't even speak decent English'.

He had little time for women, including his wife and daughter. The former was a rather ineffectual, fussy woman who both feared and admired her husband's domineering and at times violent personality. She saw her role entirely through his eyes and accepted without apparent resentment his contemptuous attitude which was mirrored in John's behaviour towards her.

PARENTAL ATTITUDES
Despite his great ambitions for John and though he doted on him, the father also enforced quite strictly those things 'which would make him a gentleman', which included good table manners, courtesy to adults and an 'insistence on your rights; that's the way to get respect from the world'. The fact that John never touched a book at home did not concern him, as he saw it as the school's job to 'give him a proper education'. Therefore he had sent him at the age of four to the most expensive prep-school in the town and made him a weekly boarder when he became seven years old. While the teaching was sound enough, it was neither sufficiently inspired nor did it aim at making up such a degree of cultural deprivation as prevailed in John's home. The boy's poor school reports had increasingly annoyed the father, who eventually agreed to the referral simply in order to get advice on a better school.

During the interview the mother rarely replied to a question, even when it was addressed to her, without tacitly seeking her husband's permission. Like him, she blamed the school rather than John for his unsatisfactory behaviour and lack of educational progress. When told of his good ability, the parents saw this simply as further proof of the school's inadequacy. Any suggestion that there was a problem, which needed to be sorted out for the sake of the whole family, was rejected out of hand by the father.

SUMMARY AND RECOMMENDATIONS

Though spoilt and adored by his uncritical, self-satisfied and aggressive father, John had received very little loving care or intellectual stimulation at home. From an early age he had had to learn to fend for himself. From both precept and example, aggressive self-assertion came to be seen by him as an acceptable pattern of behaviour, especially when it won him ascendancy and power over other boys. His inability to live up to his father's high scholastic expectations probably increased his aggressive resentment, since he could hardly be expected to understand the main reasons for this failure.

The father's emphatic refusal to countenance psychological guidance left no alternative but to close the case. Our suggestion of an alternative school was also rejected, as he suspected it of incorporating 'some of your psychological ideas'. One of his customers had told him of an 'excellent place which guarantees to get a pupil both through the 11-plus and the 13-plus common entrance examination', and he had already enrolled John there.

One had little doubt that the father would do his utmost to keep them to their guarantee, though one had serious misgivings as to the school's methods even if they were to succeed.

PROGNOSIS

It is highly doubtful that John will fulfil his intellectual promise in the scholastic sphere; he may well come to excel in other walks of life, where a combination of native wit, aggression and self-confidence pays off in terms of financial reward. There is, however, a distinct possibility that he will seriously hurt others on the way and in the process he, too, may get hurt.

5. **Jimmy,** aged 13 yr, 4 mth; M.A. 17 yr, 10 mth; I.Q. 129; R.A. 13 yr, 6 mth; S.A. 12 yr, 11 mth; A.A. 11 yr, 2 mth.

Referred by the school for being unable to cope with the work.

THE CHILD

A gentle, dreamy boy, slow to respond and lacking in confidence.
He gave the impression, accentuated by his small stature, of being
much younger than his age. Considering he came from a professional
home, his vocabulary was rather limited and his accent unexpectedly
common.

His educational attainments were barely up to his chronological age,
let alone his mental level, and in arithmetic he was more than two years
backward. As he had managed to win a special place two years previously, it looked likely that he had made only little educational progress
since then. Throughout his conversation his sister figured much more
frequently than either parent; from his comments one might have
thought that she was the elder of the two. It appeared that he had few
friends and considered many of the boys in the neighbourhood 'too
rough'.

SCHOOL

Having just managed to scrape through into a grammar school,
Jimmy had been lagging behind from the beginning. Though he gave no
trouble and, if anything, was considered to be too gentle and dependent,
his teachers had begun to wonder whether the strain of coping was not
getting too much for him. His work was increasingly falling behind,
he was becoming excessively forgetful, when reprimanded was often
near to tears and most of the time looked strained and apprehensive.
As he dreaded games and was pretty poor at them, there was nothing
from which he could gain some kudos.

FAMILY CIRCUMSTANCES

Both parents were medical researchers who had met as colleagues and
continued to work together after their marriage. They were immersed
in their studies and determined that having children would not disrupt
the pattern of their lives. In any case, they believed (or rationalised
to some extent?) that children grew up best without too much adult
supervision and interference, provided they had enough to do and
plenty of space to do it in. Therefore they bought a large house in a
rather dilapidated area of town where the proportion of lower-income,
large-size families was high.

This decision was prompted not only by the fact that they could not
have afforded a house of similar size in a better area but also by
two further considerations: their socialist principles of egalitarianism and the easy availability of domestic labour in this part of the
city.

PARENTAL ATTITUDES

Though quite fond of Jimmy and his younger sister Jean, both parents were more deeply committed to each other and to their work. While their hopes for the children seemed out of proportion to the abilities either of them had shown so far, they believed them to be 'late developers'. It was a disappointment to them that neither child was showing any signs of a scientific interest but they seemed oblivious of the fact that they had received little parental encouragement to do so. To judge from Jimmy's garbled account during the interview of his parents' occupation, the subject could not have been discussed intelligibly with him.

Jimmy's difficulties at school were thought by the parents to be due to puberty and thus merely a transient phenomenon. The fact that he had barely been up to standard when he passed the 11-plus examination they considered to be irrelevant; 'the luck of the draw and he is just not a good examination passer'.

SUMMARY AND RECOMMENDATIONS

It seemed that Jimmy and his sister were being sacrificed to their parents' scientific career and political beliefs. Insufficient parental care and company, the need to stand up for himself in a rather tough neighbourhood and school, and the lack of adult intellectual stimulation were proving an increasing strain for this rather gentle and dependent boy. His younger sister and a succession of domestic helpers could not be expected to be adequate mother substitutes. With his educational attainments only just average for his age, it was not surprising that school was becoming an increasing strain on him.

A place for remedial treatment was offered to the parents on the understanding that at least one of them would spare the time to come with him so as to ensure a weekly talk with the social worker.

SUBSEQUENT DEVELOPMENTS

It seems that the school's decision to seek outside help had been quite a jolt to the parents and that subsequent to their interview with us they did some considerable heart searching. This led them to make two decisions: first, to ask us to see their daughter, Jean, as well; second, that the mother would work shorter hours so that she could always see the children off to school and be back at home when they returned. Eventually they took a third step, namely, fitting up a laboratory at home. This was done partly to enable them to continue their work after the children had gone to bed to make up for the time they were now spending with them in the evenings; and partly so that the children could take an interest in what the parents were doing.

Jimmy was given some remedial work in arithmetic and his reading was guided to make it wider and more challenging than hitherto; for a time he was also given some help with his school work, with the full agreement of his teachers. Some advice was given to his father on how to coach Jimmy in games to help him to overcome his fears to some extent. Probably most important of all, as a result of all this unaccustomed attention, the boy's self-confidence began to increase markedly so that he no longer expected to fail before he even started. After some fifteen months it proved possible to discontinue his regular attendance and follow-up interviews indicated that the improved rate of progress was being maintained.

PROGNOSIS
Quite favourable.

6. Jean, aged 9 yr, 3 mth; M.A. 12 yr, 6 mth; I.Q. 132; R.A. 10 yr 6 mth; S.A. 9 yr; A.A. 8 yr, 8 mth.

Jimmy's sister, referred by the parents for educational backwardness.

THE CHILD
In contrast to her brother, Jean seemed older than her age, partly because of a competent, self-assured and decisive manner. Her accent was similar to Jimmy's though the actual range of her vocabulary was wider. She appeared to have a good appreciation of what she could and could not do, and would quickly dismiss a question with 'that's too hard for me; try something else'. Having to do the educational tests was a big disappointment to her as Jimmy had told her he had enjoyed himself. 'He couldn't have if he had to do sums and things,' she complained. She spoke about him in a maternal manner which was rather comical in view of their respective ages. It was clear, however, that she was the dominant character.

SCHOOL
Her attainments, too, were only about average for her age and, moreover, 'she cannot be driven to work but will concentrate well when her interest is aroused'. Apparently she was getting on better with her present teacher and her work had begun to improve. She made friends easily but had difficulty in keeping them because she tended to be rather bossy.

FAMILY CIRCUMSTANCES AND PARENTAL ATTITUDES
See previous description.

SUMMARY AND RECOMMENDATIONS

The parents had asked for Jean to be seen as they had thought she might also be underfunctioning. Though this proved to be the case, it was felt that—at least for the time being—she did not require special help. The changes which the parents were making and their increasing awareness of Jimmy's needs were likely to benefit Jean, too. Furthermore, she was doing better in school than previously and with more parental encouragement, her attitudes and hence progress might well improve further. Last, it was felt that it was good for Jimmy's morale to have a special place which helped *him* and which he did not have to share with his more competent sister.

3. Too Low Parental Expectations

The four children described in this chapter all had parents whose educational expectations were too low in relation to their child's high potential ability; in two cases this was made worse by emotional rejection, whereas in the other two there was a mixture of overindulgence and an inability to provide appropriate intellectual and cultural stimulation. With regard to the last-mentioned children, the school realised their unusually high potential but there was continual friction because their performance fluctuated so much from day to day and because their behaviour was equally unpredictable.

7. Sheila, aged 10 yr, 1 mth; M.A. 14 yr; I.Q. 134; R.A. 13 yr, 8 mth; S.A. 12 yr, 6 mth; A.A. 9 yr, 6 mth. (sister of John, No. 4 p. 27)
Referred by the family doctor for recurrent headaches.

THE CHILD
A pale, timid girl who lacked confidence to such an extent that she could not accept praise at its face value. She thought it was only being given to encourage her to keep on trying and not because she deserved it; hence her response to praise was 'You know, I really *am* trying. I always do, but I'm just not good at things like John is.' Told that she was indeed doing well, she merely gave a disbelieving smile. As in the case of John, arithmetic was her weakest school subject, where she barely reached an average level for her age; but she read well, though rather slowly. Indeed, in marked contrast to her brother, she was very slow in all her responses. Moreover, she was so uncertain of her own mind, that she often withdrew a correct answer and substituted a wrong one.

SCHOOL
Though the father had considered a private school 'for prestige reasons', he decided it was a waste of money giving a girl a good education. So Sheila was attending the local primary school, which was rather on

34

the rough side and had very large classes. She was in the B stream and described by her teacher as a 'quiet, timid girl whose work is neat but so slow she rarely manages to finish anything in time'. Because of her frequent headaches, she had been missing a fair amount of school recently. Though she was thought to be of good average ability her teachers felt it was wrong to push her 'as she is miserable enough as it is; pressure makes her worse and often leads to tears'. She was solitary, more it seemed by choice than because other children rejected her.

FAMILY CIRCUMSTANCES
As for John (see page 28).

PARENTAL ATTITUDES
The father's attitude was as domineering and contemptuous towards his daughter as to his wife. He thought the former as empty-headed as the latter, but while his wife's admiration flattered him he was antagonised by the open fear and hostility which Sheila showed towards him. Usually she preferred to be seen and not heard, but from time to time she would stand up to him. Of course, she always lost these battles of will. Recently they had tended to end in headaches accompanied by violent sickness. Eventually the mother had taken the child to the doctor and after a number of tests, which were negative, he suggested a psychological examination. Having already been to our department with John, the parents preferred this to the local Child Guidance Service.

SUMMARY AND RECOMMENDATIONS
The father found it difficult to believe that Sheila was as able as her brother but it appeared to give some satisfaction to her mother. To start with, both our suggestions were rejected by him: first, that Sheila would benefit from attending a particular convent school where classes were small and where she could be given the individual attention and gentle encouragement she so badly needed; against this, he argued he could not afford the fees. The second suggestion, that she should attend our department once a week for remedial treatment, he rejected on the grounds that he could not spare his wife from the garage and the journey was too far for Sheila to make on her own. One suspected that the father was also reluctant to have [his wife come and talk to us on her own.

A few weeks later, however, she rang up to say she had persuaded her husband to let Sheila transfer to the private school by offering to pay for it with some money left her by an aunt. She only hoped that the headaches would now disappear.

PROGNOSIS

It is difficult to assess how deeply damaged Sheila already was: on the one hand, she was still able to respond to gentle encouragement; on the other hand, she had a most pervasive sense of failure and worthlessness. Much will depend on her new school's ability to give her educational success and thus confidence to face the more difficult problem of making personal relationships.

8. Ben, Aged 11 yr, 1 mth; M.A. 16 yr, 1 mth; I.Q. 138; R.A. 12 yr, 6 mth; S.A. 10 yr, 5 mth; A.A. 9 yr, 6 mth.

Referred by the school because of limited attainments.

THE CHILD

A poised, well-spoken, almost excessively polite boy, whose conversation and sophisticated manner were far beyond his years. He considered school to be rather a bore and longed for what he saw as 'the freedom of having a private tutor, since he would appreciate that it really doesn't matter how well or badly I do'. He intended to travel as soon as he was old enough to do so by himself and commented: 'I cannot call it a hope or an ambition since I know there will be no difficulty whatsoever financially and my parents will be glad to have me off their hands. They wanted to send me to boarding school long ago but I threatened to keep running away so they gave in.' He knew that he wasn't 'as dim as some chaps, since after all I get by with doing the minimum. That's what makes them so cross, I don't try. But why should I?' Even without making any effort his attainments were about average for his age.

SCHOOL

It was the custom to let children sit both the city's selective examination and the school's own entrance examination for the senior department; if a pupil passed the former he was eligible for a bursary, should this be justified by the parents' financial situation and should they choose to let their child stay on. It gave the school the opportunity to get rid of unsuitable pupils, though in practice this was rarely done. In Ben's case they wished to do so as they considered him to be a bad influence on the other boys because of his 'utter and joyful non-competitiveness'. However, before telling the parents that his attainments were too low for making the grade in the senior school, they wanted to have an assessment of his potential and a confirmation of their own view that there were no psychological difficulties underlying his attitude.

FAMILY CIRCUMSTANCES

The father, a wealthy industrialist, had successfully extended what he had inherited from his father. He had married late, and his much younger wife, a minor film star, had a daughter of her own; since she was nine years older than Ben he was virtually an only child. When younger the father had worked (and played) quite hard but since his marriage had adopted an extremely easy-going, amused attitude to life. It pleased his wife to accept a part from time to time and 'to broaden Ben's horizon' she usually took him with her on location. In this way he picked up some serviceable Italian, Spanish and French, though he was mainly looked after by servants. The father did not believe in governesses or tutors since he considered childhood was best spent in the casual exploration of the world.

The mother did not come to the interview but was described by the father as 'a jolly, quite warmhearted girl though a bit narcissistic; you know what these show people are'.

PARENTAL ATTITUDES

It appeared that Ben was treated rather like a cute pet. From quite an early age he had been allowed to stay up for parties as long as he 'behaved himself'. This meant handing round food and cocktails, not interrupting adults too often and taking himself away without making a fuss if he got bored. As he had always been a pretty and appealing child, he was assured of a good deal of attention and admiration which his parents also enjoyed. His manners were exquisite, though at times it was open to doubt whether he was copying guests in admiration or mimicry, but since he never became blatantly obvious, his parents were amused and took it to be a sign of his general precociousness.

Right from the start he disliked going to school because he was bored and hated to sit still. As his parents were intending to send him to boarding school by the age of seven or eight, they felt he must learn to get used to classroom discipline. On the understanding (bribery?) that he would be allowed to go with his mother when she was filming, he accepted school as a necessary evil. What had set him against boarding school was a matter for conjecture but the father thought it may have been his stepsister or some older cousins. Be this as it may, he had been adamant about not wanting to go. The father felt it was unwise to put his threat of running away to the test unnecessarily and agreed to postpone a decision till Ben was older.

Though affronted by the school's demand for a psychological examination, the father had agreed to it because he felt convinced that the result would shame them into having to acknowledge that the boy was among their abler pupils.

SUMMARY AND RECOMMENDATIONS

In the event the father was proved right, since the school had not realised how able Ben was. However, from their point of view this did not alter the situation materially; they had a long waiting list and neither Ben nor his parents had made any positive contribution to the life of the school. The father did not feel inclined to have his son accepted into the senior school as a favour or on sufferance. Therefore he agreed to Ben's often repeated suggestion that he should be allowed to have a tutor for two years on the understanding that he then would 'give boarding school a try'.

PROGNOSIS

Maybe Ben's own words summed it up most succinctly. When asked what he would like to be or do when he grew up, he replied: 'When you have as much as I'll have, it doesn't really matter what I do.' Maybe he will eventually outgrow this philosophy instilled by parental indulgence?

9. **Charles,** aged 11 yr; M.A. 17 yr, 7 mth; I.Q. 150; R.A. 16 yr; S.A. 15 yr; A.A. 16 yr, 10 mth.

Referred by the school for stealing and constantly being in trouble.

THE CHILD

An attractive, physically well-developed boy with a confident, charming manner. His reactions were quick to the point of being impulsive and many of his replies showed an imaginative and unusual mind. He made a quick, easy relationship and clearly enjoyed the opportunity to talk about himself. When he found out that I knew his school had referred him because of continuous disobedience and stealing, he seemed only momentarily taken aback. Not only did he recover quickly but he added 'but do you know that they will probably expel me? This will be a record of a kind, anyhow.'

SCHOOL

Charles was one of the youngest boys who had succeeded in winning a place at this particular grammar school and became notorious within the first term. Previously he had attended a small private school where he had been suspected of being the ringleader behind many an escapade, but it had never been possible to prove his guilt. How hard the school tried is open to question, since it was realized that his outstanding ability and scholastic success would bring credit to the school. The only warning which had been passed on to the new school was that Charles was a 'high spirited, unconventional boy'.

That this was an understatement became clear within the first week. To begin with some doubt existed since he was clever in his misdeeds. When accused on suspicion, he coolly stared it out, even with the headmaster. It was many weeks before he was actually caught 'in the act'. By then a good deal of money had disappeared. All that was known until then was that on several occasions Charles had invited a number of boys to go into town with him instead of taking the school bus home (after giving them a treat in a café, he would see them all safely home by taxi); that he distributed sweets, fountain pens and other desirable 'goodies' on a lavish scale; that he began to sport an expensive waterproof, automatic watch; together with other signs of greater affluence than his home circumstances were likely to afford him.

The second galling aspect of the affair—not being able to catch him being the first—was that his school work remained excellent in a seemingly effortless, almost flaunting way. Reluctant to lose so promising a pupil the school hoped for a 'quick enough psychological solution' to be able to keep him.

FAMILY CIRCUMSTANCES
The parents looked old enough to be the boys' grandparents as in fact they could have been. The father, a civil service clerk, had been in the same job since his marriage and when Charles went to school the mother had taken up part-time clerical work to help with his fees. Both came from large families and had very much wanted to have children. On finding they were unable to have a family of their own, the parents decided to adopt a child. By that time they were well into their forties. They were not particularly choosey and Charles was in fact the first child they were offered. To their astonished delight they were told that he was the illegitimate son of an outstanding scientist but that nothing else about him could be revealed. In order 'to give him the best of everything' they decided against further adoptions which they had previously had in mind.

PARENTAL ATTITUDES
The parents, an ordinary warmhearted couple, felt a little overawed by the responsibility of bringing up what they thought of as a potential genius. They cherished him, indeed doted on him, not only because he

was quite soon showing unusual promise and passed all his milestones extremely early; but also because they felt they had to make up to him for being adopted and hence deprived of all that his own parents, particularly his brilliant father, might have done for him. And so in their eyes, he could do no wrong. They dismissed the misgivings of his teachers in the private school as 'old maids' imaginings' which was perhaps not unreasonable seeing they had never actually managed to prove anything against Charles. Though he was often disobedient and cheeky at home too, they excused this as being high-spirited. To some extent this was true since he reserved his most insolent behaviour for his teachers. Indeed, there was a code of ethics to his misdeeds: he never stole from his parents, relatives or friends but from those he knew to be better off than himself or those he regarded as his enemies; similarly, he was rarely cheeky to people he liked or respected but pompous and nagging teachers brought out the worst in him. Children were usually loyal to him—his charm, daring and generosity aroused their admiration; and with his 'enemies' he used a mixture of threats and bribery to good effect.

Even though the parents were shocked at what had happened, they felt convinced that there had been some miscarriage of justice or that he had been 'framed' because others envied his great abilities and cleverness.

SUMMARY AND RECOMMENDATIONS

Charles seemed to be an almost classic case of the spoilt, indulged and adored child of rather ineffectual, simple people whose sense of proportion had become distorted by what seemed to them a marvellous gift from heaven. They believed sincerely that there was no evil in Charles and in a sense they were right—he had grown up amoral and self-willed rather than immoral or vicious. It seemed highly unlikely that they could come to see the situation as it was and change their own handling of the boy quickly and radically enough for him to remain at home and attend his present school without further trouble. And further trouble could well mean an approved school order, were he to find himself before a Juvenile Court.

Therefore the parents were persuaded to agree to his going to a residential school for highly intelligent boys. Then in a number of preparatory talks the reasons for his being sent away were also discussed with Charles. Though he put up some resistance, saying he had learnt his lesson, one felt he half-welcomed the opportunity of help since quite spontaneously he admitted and described many of his previously undetected misdeeds.

SUBSEQUENT DEVELOPMENTS

For several years Charles came to see us during his holidays. Despite settling well after a stormy first year, he went on each occasion through the ritual of discussing whether the time had not come for him to return home. After three years his previous school became very ready to take him back when they heard that there had been no serious incidents for some time past. However, it seemed inadvisable to take the risk of returning him, possibly too early, to an environment which was virtually unchanged. Educationally he did as well as one had hoped and eventually gained university entrance with ease.

PROGNOSIS

Excellent academically and quite hopeful socially.

10. Gillian, aged 9 yr, 10 mth; M.A. 12 yr; I.Q. 127; R.A. 9 yr, 9 mth; S.A. 7 yr, 2 mth; A.A. 8 yr, 2 mth.

Referred by the school for excessive timidity.

THE CHILD

Throughout the diagnostic interview, Gillian rarely spoke in sentences, but confined herself to short phrases and, whenever possible, monosyllabic replies. She remained excessively timid and dependent on encouragement. This fearfulness was also evident in her posture and gait. She rarely looked at the examiner and derived no pleasure from her own success or praise, or from the variety of toys put at her disposal. There was little doubt that she was socially and emotionally extremely immature.

SCHOOL

Because there had been so little improvement in her timidity since she started school five years ago, the headteacher had grown increasingly concerned. Moreover, she could not see Gillian coping in the large secondary school to which she was due to go in about eighteen months time. Hence her referral.

Described as overtimid, solitary and unresponsive in class, she was said to talk to her teacher only in whispers unless there was no one else present. Though slow her written work was reasonable for her age except spelling, but she rarely took part in any oral or group activities. Coercion or even persuasion had been given up as she dissolved into tears at the slightest provocation and after an upset would be kept home by her mother.

FAMILY CIRCUMSTANCES

The father had been with the gas board since he left school at the age of fourteen and had now risen to be an inspector. The mother had been a shop assistant but stopped work on marriage. Her own mother had been a very dominant personality and opposed the marriage, ostensibly because her future husband was ten years her junior; the mother was by then thirty-seven years old. Her first two pregnancies ended in miscarriages which she felt to be a punishment for marrying despite her mother's opposition. Gillian's birth was long and difficult and she turned out to be a delicate and fretful baby.

PARENTAL ATTITUDES

The mother could not conquer her fear that she would die and so was extremely anxious and overprotective in her handling. Throughout the years her attitude had remained unchanged although Gillian was quite fit though not robust.

To her sister, four years her junior, the mother had accorded much more independence; possibly because meanwhile her own mother, whose jealousy and dislike of the baby had been intense, had died before the birth of the second child, and also because the second girl had a more assertive personality as well as a physically easier start in life.

The father, a stolid, slow, retiring man took little active interest in either of his daughters though he seemed to be quite fond of them.

SUMMARY AND RECOMMENDATIONS

The mother's guilt at disobeying her own mother had haunted her during Gillian's early life. Fearful for her well-being, particularly because of her continuing indifferent health, she was grossly overprotective towards her. This had made the child so fearful and dependent that a vicious circle set in whereby the child's apparent need of her further reinforced the mother's anxiety.

It was decided to arrange a term's observation to see whether Gillian would be able to respond to non-interpretative play therapy and to carefully supervised opportunities to mix with other children. This would also provide an opportunity to explore to what extent the mother was able and willing to co-operate with the psychiatric social worker.

SUBSEQUENT DEVELOPMENTS

Though the mother was ready to do what was best for the child, she tended to carry out suggestions to the letter. Her own personal problems, which included a lack of confidence, limited her capacity for gaining insight. However, she began to encourage Gillian to become more independent and provided opportunities for her to do so.

Gillian for her part was slower to respond in her personal development than academically. She became interested in our library and began to take books home; also she confessed to being afraid of arithmetic and welcomed being given help. Her good intelligence enabled her to make fairly rapid strides and this gave a boost to her confidence. It took much longer to get her to overcome her fears in active, messy play and in mixing with others; this she could take in small doses only. Though her play never became really spontaneous, and though at best she would only join a group if specially invited but never actively seeking the company of other children, considerable improvements took place gradually.

By the time she was due to go to the secondary school it was felt advisable to discharge her so that she could make a new start without being singled out. However, the head teacher was informed of her past difficulties both by us and her previous school—with the full agreement of the mother. The latter had been disappointed at Gillian's failure to gain a grammar school place, but was consoled by the hope of a possible transfer at the age of thirteen years. This Gillian eventually achieved.

PROGNOSIS

Reasonably good, though it is likely that she will remain rather timid and passive in her relationships, never making a first approach and easily getting hurt. Her passivity and general dependency make it very doubtful that she will ever fulfil her potential in academic work or in any future occupation.

4. Emotional Stress in the Home

The three children described in this chapter came from homes where there had been severe emotional stress over a considerable period of time. In two of the cases, moreover, neither parent was well educated and the boys' outstanding ability had not been recognised, still less been a source of pride. At school each of the three children were deeply unhappy, while their teachers were at a loss to know how to deal with them. As might be expected, the children also showed quite severe symptoms of emotional maladjustment.

11. Albert, aged 7 yr, 7 mth; M.A. 10 yr, 6 mth; I.Q. 139; R.A. 5 yr, 8 mth; S.A. 5 yr, 3 mth; A.A. below norms.

Referred by the school because of personality difficulties and serious backwardness.

THE CHILD

Most unprepossessing in appearance: small, weedy with ill-fitting spectacles and large, protruding ears; added to which Albert had a squint, an ungainly posture and walk, made worse by a limp and a quite noticeable stammer.

To establish the necessary relationship with him, prior to undertaking the psychological assessment, proved a most difficult task. He was extremely ill at ease, blushed crimson whenever he had to make a reply of more than a monosyllable, never looked me in the eye and remained tensely anxious despite explanations as to what would take place during the interview. When all reassurance proved ineffective and he was taken to the playroom in the hope that there he might become more relaxed, this was no more successful in easing his tension and lessening his painful self-consciousness. So reluctantly, I decided to make a start with the intellectual assessment.

It then transpired that it was only in response to a relatively impersonal, intellectual challenge that Albert could overcome his almost

44

crippling inability to establish contact. To say that he enjoyed thinking, might be going too far if only because some deep anxiety continued to lurk just beneath the surface; but at least he would speak much more freely and the stammer grew less incapacitating. It also became quickly apparent, that he was an exceptionally able boy and that any obtained I.Q. was bound to be an underestimate because of the restricting effect of his emotional condition.

Because it was only towards the end of the morning that Albert had become relatively relaxed and able to talk fairly spontaneously, a second diagnostic session was arranged. Before that a physical and neurological check up was carried out which indicated that the squint, limp and stammer had no detectable organic cause. Though his EEG tracing was markedly abnormal, Albert had never had any convulsive fits nor did any appear during the following twelve years; however, the EEG remained abnormal.

Despite his very good intelligence, Albert was practically a non-reader and his understanding of arithmetical processes was non-existent. Moreover, he disliked school with an intensity bordering on hatred. The main reason for this appeared to be that his extreme timidity, blushing and stammering had led to his being ridiculed and bullied by his class-mates.

At home, too, he was the odd man out among three younger sisters. According to him they were boisterous, talkative and rather stupid; at any rate they had nothing in common and he tried to keep out of their way as they too enjoyed tormenting him.

Once Albert became able to talk his wide vocabulary and power of self-expression were most impressive; all the more so considering that he came from a practically illiterate home. His critical appraisal of others—whether parents, teachers or contemporaries—was of a high order too. Though he was painfully aware of his deficiencies, especially in the educational sphere, he also realised that compared with contemporaries his general knowledge and particularly his scientific understanding were far superior.

The puzzling question was how or where he had acquired these. The answer turned out to be simple: by listening to the radio.

SCHOOL

Albert was due to go up to the junior school at the end of the term and the headmistress feared he would completely fail to cope there. Hence her decision to refer him for psychological examination. She described him as the strangest child she had ever dealt with: 'You cannot get through however hard you try; his attainment is low enough for an E.S.N.

school and he hardly makes any contact with the other children; yet here and there he comes out with an extraordinary remark when he happens to be alone with his teacher or no one else is listening. But in class he refuses to take part in oral work and his ability to cope with written work is practically non-existent. His teachers find him wholly unresponsive; they are aware of his being completely rejected by other children.'

The headmistress added that she had become concerned about him in his very first term but did not believe such a dull child could benefit from psychological help. Since the only other alternative to her mind was a residential E.S.N. school (a day one not being available in the area) she was reluctant to take action as she was against sending so young a child away from home even if it was an unsatisfactory one.

Teaching methods used in the school were rather rigid and in reading the approach was exclusively a phonic one. This was believed to be the most suitable for the less academically able child for whom the school largely catered. Discipline and general classroom management were similarly old-fashioned so that there was little opportunity for individual guidance and maximum use was made of competition. For a child like Albert this was misery since he found himself invariably at the bottom of any mark list.

Nor could he find relief in P.E., games or art, since his clumsiness, poor co-ordination and awkward gait presented serious handicaps. Thus he had no escape in school from constant failure and isolation. 'A really pathetic boy who doesn't know how to smile' was the class teacher's summary.

FAMILY CIRCUMSTANCES

The father, an unskilled labourer, had difficulty in holding down a steady job, partly because he had a rather quick temper; so the mother worked as a cleaner to supplement the family income, but she too was temperamentally rather erratic and in and out of jobs. The father's mentally defective brother lived with the family and his dirty habits, incontinence and childishly demanding ways caused much quarrelling and recrimination between the parents; however, the father refused to let him go to a mental hospital. Albert had to share a bedroom with this uncle who distressed and disgusted him. The youngest sister slept in the parents' bedroom and the other girls in the living room. Thus the house was not only overcrowded but there was perpetual chaos; the mother was chronically 'trying to catch up', partly because she was a poor manager and partly because she simply had too much to cope with.

PARENTAL ATTITUDES

The handling of all the children was very unpredictable and inconsistent. There was a fair amount of shouting and ineffectual slapping which appeared to have little effect on the girls but worried and upset Albert. He was clearly the mother's favourite because 'he was a boy and so different from his three sisters'. The father's attitude was a mixture of bemusement and irritation. The former was caused by Albert asking questions to which he could not find answers; for example, at the age of three years Albert went through a period of not going to sleep for long hours and showing evident distress about it. Eventually he said to his exasperated father: 'If only you would tell me where I go to when I have to go to sleep, then I could try harder.' The irritation was caused by his son's 'stubborn, sullen and superior ways'.

The three girls seemed quite ordinary and were making reasonable progress at school, compared with Albert's severe backwardness. 'Yet I know he isn't stupid,' was the father's comment, 'he sits for hours listening to the wireless. There are rows about it because he wants everyone to shut up. His favourite programme is science survey which I don't understand myself.' Both parents were worried lest he be sent to the 'daft school'.

SUMMARY AND RECOMMENDATIONS

There could be no doubt that Albert was an exceptionally able as well as a seriously maladjusted boy. The long-term solution would probably have to be boarding school because his home was so incapable of meeting his needs; currently it was particularly harmful because of the effect which the mentally handicapped uncle was having on the boy. However, we shared the school's view that it was undesirable to remove such a young child from his family. Therefore, Albert was accepted for remedial treatment and play therapy though there was little likelihood of basically modifying his home conditions.

SUBSEQUENT DEVELOPMENT

After several months' work with the parents, especially the father, it was agreed that for the sake of Albert and his mother, admission to a hospital should be sought for the uncle. It then took another year to bring this about. Meanwhile the boy had 'discovered' reading. Switching over to a combination of a look-and-say and kinaesthetic approach had quite dramatic results: within a matter of a few months Albert became a fluent reader and revelled in his new-found skill. Just as radio before, so books now opened new worlds to him. However, his spelling improved at a much slower rate and his handwriting remained a problem to him for many years; it was ill-formed, slow and cumbersome. Thus it constituted a barrier between his excellent vocabulary and power of speech (the stammer gradually disappeared) on the one hand, and his incapacity to cope with the mechanics of writing on the other. This discrepancy was likely to constitute an increasingly serious handicap as he grew older.

Once he became confident enough to converse freely, the real extent of his facility with words and ideas became apparent. For example, children were given free milk during their two-hour session with us. Albert's comment on this was 'I regard it as extraordinarily generous of the authorities, considering this is not an ordinary, educational establishment.' No wonder that when eventually he became able to talk with other children, he got himself nicknamed Professor. Arithmetic remained a closed book to him mainly because he was bored by the subject. Though there was also some slow improvement in his capacity to cope with life's stresses and strains, these remained too difficult for him to surmount entirely. His parents' personal and intellectual inadequacy; the squalor and chronic muddle of his home; the lack of privacy on the one hand and of opportunity for widening his horizons on the other; all these limitations were too severe, particularly for a child who had become so vulnerable because of the deprivation and emotional stress he had experienced from very early on in his life.

Though scholastically he was catching up, he had too much leeway to make up to succeed in the selection examination; moreover, he was a poor examinee, getting extremely worked up and hence slower than ever in his written efforts. However, it proved possible to obtain a place for him in a residential school for maladjusted but highly intelligent children. There he went for the following seven years. He made good progress but always slipped back, especially in adjustment, during school holidays. Throughout them his mother would spoil him 'for not being with us normally', to the extent of letting him stay in bed every day as long as he wished, not expecting him to give any help, and not even suggesting he should do at least some homework—she knew he was expected to complete a number of assignments and essays. Thus he slipped back all too readily into the passivity, aimlessness and chaos of the parental home.

Eventually he obtained several O levels but kept failing A level examinations until the local authority decided that payment of fees could no longer continue.

First of all, Albert obtained a post in a solicitor's office, but he walked out after a few weeks because he became bored and lonely. Then he tried his hand at photography but did not like it. Next came training for market research and then the export trade. When we last heard of him he was still very unsettled and unfortunately the periods without a job were becoming longer.

PROGNOSIS

Not hopeful. Attempts were made to find a hostel for him so that he could live away from home. However, both the parents as well as he himself were anxious for him to do so. While he had never completely slipped back during the past eleven years there had always been adults available to counteract the demoralising influence of his home conditions. It now looked as if without such support he would not be able to make out despite his very high intelligence.

12. Paul, aged 13 yr, 5 mth; M.A. 21 yr, 10 mth; I.Q. 156; educational test results: all above the norms.

Referred by the school for complete non-conformity.

THE CHILD

A tall, thin and pale boy with an adult manner; rather detached and arrogantly aware of his exceptional ability yet without any pleasure in it. Once he dropped his defences, it became apparent that he was deeply unhappy: his health had always been indifferent and he suffered from asthma; he was convinced that like his eldest brother he would die young; his parents were living a cat and dog life when together; ever since he could remember one or the other would walk out for a time; he had never had a friend, partly because he dared not ask anyone home as his parents went on brawling regardless of who was there and partly because he had never found anyone who shared his one passionate interest, mathematics; now matters were worse because he was passing through adolescence with all its doubts, fears and uncertainties.

Having had to put up at home with constant rows and being shouted at, this was the one thing he would not accept from others. In his junior school he had been relatively happy. There his outstanding ability had been recognised and because of it what were called his 'eccentricities' had been tolerated; in any case, it had been a child-centred regime with a minimum of rules and punishment. Consequently he had regarded school as a haven of tranquillity. As a result he had given of his best even when he was not particularly interested because the pride they took in him made him want to please.

Trouble began within the first week in the grammar school. Paul said

3

he had always been absentminded but particularly so when there was a bad row going on at home. 'I know I should by now be inured to it but I still can't take it, it makes me tremble all over.' When on two consecutive occasions he had forgotten his plimsolls, he was accused of insolence and harshly punished. This started his resentment which built up during the coming weeks as attempts were made 'as I see it to take me down a peg or two. They were into me for everything. Even for using my own way of solving a mathematical problem when I arrived at the correct solution from first principles and I was not even allowed to demonstrate how I had done it.'

This final injustice of not giving him credit for independent thought began the first systematic rebellion on which he had ever embarked, since he was basically a gentle, dreamy and retiring boy. Passive resistance became his motto from now on. And that was how eventually he was referred by his school. 'Everything has been tried to ensure a minimum of conformity', the letter stated, 'but he is quite impervious to any punishment which has been imposed. We are anxious to keep him as he promises to be quite an outstanding mathematician and chess player.'

THE SCHOOL

As they saw it he was 'deliberately flouting every school rule' and doing so openly and apparently unconcernedly. At the same time his manner remained studiedly polite and his work deteriorated only a little—still keeping him near the top of the top form. He 'refused to listen to reason' and neither parent had come to see the headmaster when asked to do so. The school was unaware that at the time in question the father had been again 'absent' from home and that the mother was too scared to face an admittedly very imposing headmaster.

FAMILY CIRCUMSTANCES

The father had fought with the Polish forces during the war and considered this to have been the happiest time of his life. He had never settled down afterwards and had turned his hand to a great variety of jobs. At present he was doing well, owning two flourishing cafés. When doing well, he was generous and refused to save even though such periods were invariably followed by hard times, so hard that he had been in prison several times. He was an explosive, domineering, swashbuckling man who still spoke broken English 'because he just couldn't be bothered'. He taunted his wife that his accent was superior to her common East End one and he would not let her forget that she had been a waitress when he had 'picked her out of the gutter'—perhaps an exaggeration, but he was undoubtedly the more intelligent and educated of the two.

The mother, a peroxide blonde, who affected rather girlish ways, seemed both to despise and to fear her husband. She openly relished provoking his temper and though she knew what he was capable of when roused, kept goading him on. If she had gone too far, especially in front of others, she would leave home to stay with her mother or sister but with every intention of returning. That was why she had never taken either boy with her. The older son had left home at sixteen and they rarely heard from him. 'He was as fed up with the rows as Paul is.' There seemed to be some mystery attached to the death of the oldest boy and both parents refused to talk about it.

The family frequently moved house since according to the father's current state of affluence they would live in an opulently appointed house or in a tiny basement flat 'and everything in between of course'. This seemed to be a source of amusement to the father who hated nothing more than 'a quiet life—plenty of time for that when you are dead'; but to the mother and Paul squalid conditions were humiliating.

PARENTAL ATTITUDES

Both parents were inconsistent but in different directions. The father was at times overdemanding because he was proud of his clever son and impatient with his dreamy, secretive ways; but at other times he lost interest and would ignore him completely. The mother alternated between spoiling and nagging, particularly during periods when her husband left her. Paul had learned to live with these swings without showing much outward reaction. This equanimity riled his parents who were largely unaware of the price the boy was paying for it in terms of nervous energy and periodic bouts of despair.

SUMMARY AND RECOMMENDATIONS

The school situation had reached the point of no return as Paul was adamant that he would not knuckle under: 'There is nothing more they can do to me now, I have been through all the hoops.' He himself insisted on a change of school and seemed not averse to our suggestion that he might be finding life easier if he lived away from home, at least for a year or two.

At first the parents protested bitterly of 'losing their third son'. It was difficult to judge how genuine this protestation was since each was blaming the other form aking Paul's home life unbearable. Eventually it was agreed that this was the best way out of the present impasse.

SUBSEQUENT DEVELOPMENTS

A place was found for Paul in a boarding school for very able children who took a small number of maladjusted boys. There he settled down well. Though after a couple of years his previous school tried hard to persuade the parents to let him return, and they were also anxious that he should come to live at home, he agreed with us that he was under far less strain than he had been for years. Even his physical health had improved and these days he was rarely even wheezy.

PROGNOSIS

Paul did so well that he had the choice of both Oxford and Cambridge. However, he chose London University as he had developed a great interest in music and wanted to be 'near the centre of things'.

Academically he is likely to be outstanding all round, but his mathematical gift holds great promise. However, his health became indifferent again after he left school and he grew prone to periods of deep depression. One fears that he may have been exposed at too early an age and for too long a time to the unstable and unpredictable temperaments of his parents.

13. Betty, aged 6 yr 6 mth; M.A. 9 yr 6 mth; I.Q. 149; R.A. 10 yr; S.A. 8 yr, 6 mth; A.A. 6 yr, 6 mth.

Referred by the school for being beyond control and destructive.

THE CHILD

Faced with an attractive serious-faced six-year-old, it was difficult to believe that a school could find her unmanageable. However, once she had left her parents, her determination to dominate the situation soon became evident. Betty began the interview by declaring that she had no intention of answering stupid questions. On being told that I did not think my questions would be stupid, she scowled and gave the table a vicious kick. Then she pulled a book out of her pocket and began to read. So I busied myself with some papers and told her to let me know when she was ready to talk to me. This also displeased her and she declared she had nothing to say to me. I suggested that in that case there was no point in our sitting here together as I had other things to do.

Only when we had reached the waiting room door, did she accept that I would not persuade or coerce her. Then at last she conceded that having come all this way she might as well see what I wanted her to do.

This prelude to Betty's psychological examination contained all the ingredients of her present difficulties: a determination to dominate her environment, especially the adults in it; a desire to impress; her need to test out how far she could go and whether she had the power to intimidate; and an urge to destroy and to provoke punishment.

Thus the whole interview became a battle of wits: on my part, to avoid a head-on confrontation which might force her into outright defiance; on her part, to make me lose patience or force an issue. Though we got through the morning without either happening, it proved a very exhausting business. It was clear that such a situation could not be contained day in and day out under normal classroom conditions.

SCHOOL

This was the fifth school which Betty had attended in the space of fifteen months. The first two had been state infant schools, the rest private schools. The parents' hope that the smaller classes in the latter would enable teachers to cope with Betty, had proved illusory. In each school the pattern had been the same: uncontrollable temper tantrums; destructiveness of other children's possessions and of school equipment; and a constant need to dominate the scene. Though her present school thought she was quite bright (when she chose to do some work), her attainments were felt to be a minor issue compared with her self-willed and aggressive behaviour, which was a constant threat to all concerned. 'It is unnerving to have her in one's class' was the unanimous verdict, after she had been tried with both older and younger children.

FAMILY CIRCUMSTANCES

Betty's father was a research chemist whose energies and interests were divided between his scientific work and local politics. He was an apparently quiet, gentle, very controlled man whose reaction to being provoked by his wife was to use icy sarcasm.

The mother was a mathematics teacher and a highly intellectual woman. She considered her husband an ineffectual, weak man and attributed his professional and political success to his being 'such a gentleman'. In her eyes gentleness was a sign of 'abdicating intellectual responsibility for improving the condition of man'. Making no secret of her deep disappointment in him and their marriage, she invited his sarcastic rejoinders by a critically destructive and openly hostile manner.

PARENTAL ATTITUDES

The mother recognised that Betty was unusually precocious. For example, she was able to read *The Times* at the age of four years. Why she should have wanted her to do so remained unclear. At the same time, the mother considered Betty to be unusually self-willed and so she determined 'to make her recognise who is boss' by being strict and punitive. This led to some appalling battles, since the mother made it a principle 'never to give in and never to be beaten'. As the mother seemed obsessionally house-proud, this alone provided an area of constant conflict; not that Betty was exceptionally careless or untidy, but this was not good enough for the mother's exacting standards.

Right from the beginning the father had opted out of these struggles. He doted on his only child and was indulgently overprotective to counteract what he considered to be his wife's overstrict and unrealistic expectations.

Betty responded more readily to her father which led the mother to accuse him of bribing the child by appearing more affectionate and gentle than herself. Because of the mother's jealous possessiveness he chose to play a minor part in the child's life and to be away from home; he felt it to be in the child's interest to avoid arguments about her, even if it was inevitable that she should witness some (often bitter) disagreements about other matters.

SUMMARY AND RECOMMENDATIONS

The three main strands which had led to the present situation seemed fairly clear: a domineering, obsessional woman determined to subdue both husband and daughter; a father just as determined in his own quiet way to preserve his freedom of action and independence of mind; and an able, strong-willed child caught up in their struggle for dominance and possession. She in turn attempted to impose her own will on teachers and other children, acting out the behaviour pattern which she was witnessing daily at home. Added to this, she had remained insufficiently stretched intellectually both at home and at school and so she devoted her lively mind and imagination to exciting 'diversionary activities'.

All the parents were prepared to accept was advice regarding Betty's future schooling. They completely rejected the idea that the problem could only be tackled indirectly and that it depended in the first place on their willingness to face what had become of their marriage. Even an exploratory interview with a psychiatrist or marriage guidance counsellor was refused. Hence there was little that could be done to help Betty, although a possible school was suggested. With the parents' permission a full report was given to them prior to the child's admission. She was to be kept fully occupied with work appropriate to her attainment and capacity and, as far as possible, head-on clashes with her should be avoided. However, the family moved away from the district after a few weeks which was a pity since Betty had settled better in this school than any of the others.

PROGNOSIS
None too hopeful.

5. The Effect of Physical Handicap

The three children described in this chapter had various physical handicaps but in each case the home was loving and supporting so that the child had developed a basically good and resilient personality. However, they were not so fortunate at school—at least to begin with. Two of the children were thought to be slow and backward and this failure to recognise their good potential ability led inevitably to unhappiness and to a dislike of school. Had classes been smaller or the teachers concerned more sensitive to the signs of good intelligence other than the conventional one of high attainments, the children could have been spared a good deal of stress. In each case, too, the parents believed in their child—though not necessarily recognising his excellent potential—and were willing to do battle on his behalf.

14. Toby, aged 9 yr, 9 mth; M.A. 13 yr, 4 mth; I.Q. 133; R.A. 7 yr, 2 mth; S.A. 6 yr, 8 mth; A.A. 9 yr, 6 mth.

Referred by the school for an assessment of his ability.

THE CHILD

At the beginning of the interview, Toby was somewhat reserved and shy. Soon, however, this was replaced by a most engaging, sensible and poised manner, revealing also a sense of humour and a maturity of outlook. Because of his cleft palate, it was at times difficult to understand him; however, he willingly repeated what he had said and did not desist from making spontaneous comments. Praise and success greatly pleased him; when faced with difficult problems he made persistent efforts to solve them and was able to accept failure in good part.

On testing, he was found to do considerably better on non-verbal, practical and visuomotor problems and was rather weaker on the verbal side. Educationally he was severely retarded, especially considering that he proved to be an able boy: his reading was two and a half years below his actual age and his spelling three years below it;

in arithmetic, his standard, though somewhat better, was still only average for his age.

SCHOOL

The headmistress, who had referred the boy, stated that he had been thought of as a very slow learner until a young, newly qualified teacher recently began to take an interest in him. To begin with she had felt sorry for him since he seemed timid and anxious, had a bad speech defect, few friends and an obvious fear of teachers and school life in general. He never took part in oral work and often seemed 'miles away'. Well behaved and very retiring, he easily escaped attention. However, she grew so concerned about his refusal to make any spontaneous approach to her, that she went out of her way at break and lunch-times to talk with him. After a while she began to suspect that he might be deaf; a specialist examination confirmed high frequency deafness and he was fitted with a hearing aid. Then she came to think that his vision might be defective and once again she was proved correct and he was given glasses. After two terms in her class, he had grown far less timid and worried, was willingly participating in oral work and eager to talk about his interests. The quality of some of his contributions made her wonder whether he might not be quite intelligent despite his poor educational attainments and despite the opinions held by his previous, more experienced teachers. As the headmistress appreciated the interest this young teacher had taken in Toby, she agreed to refer him to our department for a diagnostic examination.

FAMILY CIRCUMSTANCES

Both parents had won 'scholarships' but family circumstances had prevented them taking advantage of a grammar school education. Leaving school at fifteen, father became apprenticed to an engineering firm with whom he had remained except for war service. Mother did secretarial work until marriage. Their first-born, a thirteen-year-old girl, had always done well educationally and was now attending a grammar school. The family seemed to be happy and closely knit, with both parents sharing and stimulating their children's interests. Brother and sister were said to get on well together. No unfavourable comparisons had ever been made between their widely differing educational achievements.

The only sorrow and anxiety had centred around Toby's physical disability: he had been born with a cleft palate which had necessitated seven operations before the age of five years and there were more to come. The parents had always insisted on visiting him daily even though it led to quite a battle, especially with one hospital. Though his speech had become increasingly intelligible, the last operation had made it rather worse and continued speech therapy seemed to have little effect. The family's disappointment was all the greater since it had been hoped that no more operations would be needed; now that decision had been reversed and Toby knew he was facing yet further surgery.

PARENTAL ATTITUDES

Toby was a much wanted baby and when told of his handicap, the mother said she felt she would 'love him even more because he would have to suffer'. Not only did she realise that he would need all the encouragement and support that she and the father could give him, but she was also aware of the danger of overprotecting and smothering him. The parents accepted that learning to talk would be a particularly difficult task for him and therefore gave him plenty of stimulation to bring on his speech. They vividly described their frequent dilemma about how long to continue urging him to say something more clearly and when to accept what he was producing, especially since they nearly always knew what he wanted to say. However, until he started school, neither parent thought of him as a particularly dull child.

Right from the beginning Toby did not take to school. This dislike assumed serious proportions when he went up to the junior school: he clearly was reluctant to go, had frequent tummy-aches and bouts of sickness, slept badly during term time and was obviously most unhappy. The mother became torn between allowing him to stay at home and making him go despite his pleas; she also became worried lest she had unwittingly overprotected him and given him so much love that he was now afraid to venture out and face competition. Feeling that perhaps he had been given praise at home too readily for his efforts, she taxed him with laziness and letting the family down when he brought home a particularly damning school report (which finished 'he could at least try harder'). At this Toby broke down, weeping bitterly, protesting that he had always tried and if only she would teach him at home, he would not mind working longer than at school and having no play time at all. The mother then realised the full extent of the boy's unhappiness. She went to see the head and class teacher, explaining that she and her husband had no educational ambitions and only wished that Toby should grow up feeling not too different from other boys; that they did not mind his being at the bottom of the lowest stream as long as he was reasonably happy at school.

Toby had started the third year in the juniors with the new young teacher previously mentioned. After only a few weeks with her, his attitude changed quite dramatically: he began to talk at home about what he was doing at school, wanted to take things to contribute to class projects, joyously mentioned that his teacher was giving him extra help so that he was now getting a few stars and that he in turn was being allowed to do jobs and run errands for her. The mother said one of her unhappiest moments came when, shortly after he had been fitted with a hearing aid, she was told he would also have to wear glasses. She felt that circumstances were increasingly singling out Toby as being, and indeed looking, different from other children. Yet he himself accepted these new burdens better than the parents had dared to hope; later they learned that his teacher had briefed his classmates not to comment on these new aids.

SUMMARY AND RECOMMENDATIONS

Toby had been enabled by wise and loving parental handling to develop into a mentally healthy child with a good personality structure. Despite severe physical handicaps, hospitalisations and the shocks of frequent surgical interventions, his emotional and social growth had been normal and his capacity for making personal relationships had remained un-impaired. Probably because he had taught himself to lip-read, his partial deafness had escaped attention at home. At school the situation became very different. Of course such a handicapped child presents a difficult problem to a teacher, particularly if she has to deal with a class of fifty children. But it is also easy to see why Toby should have become such an unhappy failure in school: unable to make himself understood easily or quickly; unable to hear properly and prevented from lip-reading by the teacher's normal movements around the classroom; being scolded for laziness as his work became increasingly slower (educational back-wardness being inevitably cumulative unless tackled constructively); bewildered by his failure and deeply upset by his family's disapproval. Considering the daily and cumulative impact of these experiences over a number of years on a sensitive and able child, it suggests considerable stability that a more serious breakdown was avoided. Despite having lived at school in a chronic state of insecurity, beset by failure with new experiences, lack of praise and recognition, he could yet respond com-paratively quickly to a sympathetic and understanding teacher. No doubt continued parental support and the continued enjoyment of a happy family life contributed to avoiding his sinking into complete despair or retreat.

Both the headmistress and class teacher attended the case conference. Though Toby was likely to benefit from remedial teaching in our department, there were a number of contra-indicatory circumstances:

he had already had much specialist attention; he was still attending a speech therapy clinic and also missing school not infrequently because of various re-examinations at the hospital, so that an additional weekly half-day's absence might be unwise; lastly there was no urgency to improve his attainments since he seemed to stand no chance of passing the 11 plus examination in a year's time. It was decided to watch his progress through six-monthly re-examinations in our department. Now that his good ability was known, his teacher was hoping to bring about quickened progress without fear of expecting too much from him. The headmistress decided to let Toby stay with the same mistress even though it would mean promotion to a B stream in the following year.

SUBSEQUENT DEVELOPMENTS

One factor everyone had underestimated was the effect of the boy's changed attitude to learning on his determination to succeed. He asked his teacher for homework and got up every morning at six o'clock to do it; he persuaded his parents and teacher to give him private coaching during the Easter and summer holidays (even offering to pay for it out of his pocket money!). Periodic re-examinations showed excellent acceleration in his rate of learning. But as he had to make up such leeway, I tried to persuade him that time was too short for him to catch up sufficiently to succeed in the examination on which he had now set his heart; I did this in an endeavour to avoid too deep a disappointment but he would not accept what seemed sound educational sense. In the event he proved to be the wiser: he won a place to a technical school where he did very well indeed. Eventually he became articled to an accountant and continued to pass successfully all the necessary examinations, in each case 'first go'. At the early age of twenty-one, he passed his finals and was admitted as an Associate of the Institute of Chartered Accountants.

Throughout the years he kept in touch with me, sending me school reports, photos and a press cutting when he went to Buckingham Palace to receive a Duke of Edinburgh award.

PROGNOSIS

Excellent despite, or perhaps partly because of, his various handicaps. Everyone who comes into contact with him admires not only his determination to compete on equal terms and to have no allowances made; but also his warm, responsive, compassionate attitude towards others and the complete absence of self-pity. Though his speech is by no means perfect it is unlikely to impede his progress in his chosen career. Good though his ability is, he has sharpened its cutting edge by making use of every ounce of it and of his personal qualities to overcome his disabilities.

15. Martin, aged 5 yr, 11 mth; M.A. 11 yr, 1 mth; I.Q. 175; R.A. 10 yr; S.A. 9 yr, 2 mth; A.A. 7 yr, 1 mth.

Referred by the mother because of the boy's dislike of school.

THE CHILD

A sturdy, well built little boy whose lively conversation and penetrating reasoning soon dispelled the first impression that his mother had overestimated his ability. Though he did not seem to be unduly precocious, he had great self-confidence and poise. Once he realised that I was interested to listen to him, he gave lengthy and quite fascinating replies to the questions put to him. In the manner of young but very intelligent children, he was quite unaware of the unusual quality of his responses and quite unselfconscious in expressing his opinions on an uncommonly wide range of subjects.

The level he had reached in the basic subjects was extraordinarily high, considering that the mother insisted she had not coached him and that he had certainly not been taught at this level in his school.

SCHOOL

The report received from the headmistress made it patently clear that in her view a fuss was being made about nothing and that Martin's mother was overestimating her son's ability 'a not uncommon occurrence in this district'.

Martin was considered to be an average little boy who was simply taking rather longer to settle down than was usual. He was described as quiet, withdrawn and somewhat unsociable 'probably because his mother has tended to overprotect and spoil him'. He was said to be good at arithmetic but below average in reading. In view of his outstandingly high attainment in both this subject and spelling, this was a most surprising assessment.

FAMILY CIRCUMSTANCES

The father was an accountant and the mother had trained as a teacher and hoped one day to return to work as she had very much enjoyed it. In fact it was because she had visited our department during her training and listened to a case conference that she felt we might be able to help. The parents gave the impression of a happy, affectionate couple who thoroughly enjoyed their children. They had similar ideas on their upbringing and discipline, imposed a minimum of sensible rules and spent a good deal of time sharing interests with the family. There were also two girls, Martin being the oldest. The mother took a very relaxed attitude over housework saying 'a spotless house means miserable children'.

PARENTAL ATTITUDES

During his early years, Martin had suffered a good deal from catarrh as well as middle ear and bronchial trouble; so much so that the parents had seriously considered moving to a different part of the country. However, they hesitated because they had elderly parents living in the area. Also as Martin grew older these conditions had improved except that he tended to get rather frequent and heavy colds when he seemed to have hearing difficulties. The specialist had told the parents that such 'intermittent deafness' was not unusual but that there was no treatment for it.

As in every other way Martin was developing well and could be considered quite advanced for his age, the parents did not worry about this difficulty. Though Martin was clearly ready for school long before the age of five years, pressure on places made it impossible for him to be admitted earlier. Despite his desire to be taught, the mother refused to do so as she feared she might confuse him if different methods would be used once he went to school. Then she discovered that he had learned to read and spell by himself, presumably with the aid of being told the names of street signs, labels on cartons and captions of his favourite programmes in the *Radio Times* and on TV.

Starting school was a joyful event, but after the first week he became very dissatisfied ''cause we do no work, just playing all the time, I can do this better at home, there's more room for one thing and more interesting toys for another'. She reassured him that this would soon change once everyone had got used to school but his complaints about being bored and wasting his time grew increasingly plaintive as the weeks went by. By the end of the first term things were going from bad to worse and Martin was asking daily to be allowed to stay at home 'to do some real work like sums or spellings'.

Having rightly felt that Martin was more than ready for school, the parents' disappointment was all the greater that after so short a time, he had developed this intense dislike, saying he was bored and there were many more interesting things to do at home. Being herself a trained teacher, the mother was puzzled and decided to get to the bottom of it.

Both parents had always taken a constructive interest in their children's development and education and hoped they would do reasonably well; however, they considered it harmful to 'make a big thing of the

11-plus like most people do in this district and to bribe children with all kinds of promises if they make it'.

Therefore, the mother was all the more affronted by the response of the headmistress when she went to have a talk about Martin's dislike of school. She was treated like 'a fussy mum' and told that children may take quite a time to settle down at school. When she explained that she knew this, being a trained, experienced teacher herself, and that more-over Martin had very much looked forward to starting school, both observations were practically ignored. Instead the headmistress closed the interview by saying 'I would suggest you dismiss from your mind any thought of the 11-plus—there just isn't a chance. But if you stop worrying about him, there is no reason why he should not make quite satisfactory progress.' This parting shot so infuriated the mother that she quite forgot to mention Martin's intermittent deafness as she had intended to do. Her annoyance was caused as much by the fact that a school should begin to apply the yardstick of the selection examination at this early age as by the dogmatic certainty with which the pro-nouncement had been made. The injustice of the comment, as she genuinely had not even started to think about the examination, only struck her later and added to her anger.

SUMMARY AND RECOMMENDATIONS

Though the parents had believed Martin to be quite a bright boy, they were delighted to learn that his ability was exceptionally high. Since his attainments were also outstanding for his age, one could confidently predict that he should easily succeed in the selection examination— which he subsequently did. Why then had things gone wrong at school? Ironically enough it looked as if the main reason was its 'progressive-ness', applied in too rigid and unimaginative a way.

In an area known for the generally high socio-economic level of the population, the consequently high educational ambitions of the parents and the good 11-plus results of the junior school, the headmistress prided herself on resisting the pressure to run 'a forcing house'. Instead she genuinely believed in the value of an informal, gradual approach to formal learning. Children whom she considered to be 'high flyers' she promoted from the reception class after the first term, but in that class little opportunity was given to children who were ready or already able to read and who in any case did not have much need for informal, wholly individual play but could cope with group activities, both in play and work.

Martin's boredom and disillusionment with school had been inter-preted by a rather inexperienced young teacher as lack of ability. In addition, his intermittent deafness made him unable to respond on occasions when he was affected by it, particularly in the hurly-burly of a constantly 'active' classroom.

It seemed providential that the mother had forgotten to mention this handicap since it provided a face-saving device for the headteacher. With the agreement of the parents we recommended that Martin be allowed to 'jump a whole year' so that he could be placed in the top class where much more formal work was done in preparation for transfer to the junior school. The grounds for this proposal were said to be that in this much quieter atmosphere, Martin's deafness would be far less of a handicap. At first the headteacher resisted this suggestion as she felt it was wrong to make a child stay in the same class for two years in succession. We offered to discuss the matter with the headmaster of the junior school with whom we had a close working relationship. He agreed to accept Martin a year early so that he would not have to spend two years in the same class. Finally, honour was satisfied when we asked the aural surgeon to confirm in a letter to the infant school head that Martin's condition made a 'quiet class room' desirable.

SUBSEQUENT DEVELOPMENTS

The infant school was pleased to report that Martin had responded well to being moved up and his latent ability was now 'beginning to show'. Greatly to the parents' credit, they showed enough forbearance not to point out the true facts. They realised that for the boy's sake, it was advisable to let the school take credit for his 'improvement and greater will to work'. Relations between the mother and the headteacher remained somewhat strained; as the two younger children would have to go to the same school, the mother never demurred when the head referred to Martin as 'a late developer' on hearing how brilliantly he was doing in the junior and subsequently the grammar school.

The family kept in touch for many years and then Martin himself visited and wrote letters to tell us about his progress. At the time of writing he is trying to decide whether to read psychology or medicine at university, having collected an impressive number of A levels.

PROGNOSIS

Excellent.

16. Jack, aged 10 yr, 9 mth; M.A. 16 yr, 2 mth; I.Q. 142; R.A. 13 yr, 8 mth; S.A. 11 yr, 6 mth; A.A. 12 yr, 4 mth.

Referred by a plastic surgeon for the psychological after-effects of a street accident.

THE CHILD

A rather obese, depressed boy who became tearful when discussing how his accident had affected his life. He had been quite athletic and outstandingly good at football, cricket and swimming. He had had many friends and apparently a good deal of freedom from parental supervision. Now he was unable to take part in physical activities, partly because he was still partially paralysed on his left side and partly because his mother 'doesn't let me out of her sight now'. He had been good at his school work too, but 'now I am so slow I just never finish anything in time'. In eight months' time he was due to sit for the selection examination and was sure he would fail.

As he grew confident that I was 'not on his mother's side', as he put it, he poured out the whole story. And very truthful and perceptive it turned out to be when facts were checked both with his parents and the hospital. Jack realised it was almost a miracle that he survived and he was profoundly grateful to the surgeons and the hospital staff. Indeed, his appreciation was quite unchildlike. He remembered little of his actual recovery except that he was unable to speak for a long time.

At first he despaired, fearing that his friends would not want to have any more to do with him 'seeing I am practically a cripple'. In fact his mother proved to be the greater obstacle. Now Jack was torn by a conflict to which he could see no solution: on the one hand he felt guilty at having caused her so much anguish and was aware of the great care and love she and the whole family had lavished on him; for example: 'They came to visit me in hospital every day while some people had no one for days and days; and they had a long journey I found out later.' On the other hand, he felt, 'mollycoddled when I know I am almost all right but she won't let me get out by myself'.

THE SCHOOL

Before the accident, he had been a lively, active, cheerful boy who was well liked by his teachers and extremely popular with other boys, 'a born leader'. Though competition to gain entry into the one and only Catholic grammar school was stiff, and the parents would not let him go to any other but preferred the secondary modern Catholic school, the staff had been confident that Jack would succeed in gaining a place. Now his chances were slim indeed 'unless the miracle we are praying for will happen'.

FAMILY CIRCUMSTANCES

The family were Irish Catholics and though all the children, two girls and three boys (including Jack) had been born in England, they all

spoke of Ireland as home. The father was a labourer and the mother
had worked as a cleaner but stopped this after Jack's accident. He was
the youngest of the family and had been allowed more freedom than the
others. In the mother's words 'I suppose as you have more of them you
get less worried and anyhow, Jack had always been an independent lad
but sensible and steady as well.'

The family lived a long way from the Catholic junior school the boy
was attending but a school-bus was provided; Jack only had to cross
one main road and it was while he was doing so on a pedestrian crossing
that he was knocked down by a hit-and-run driver. There was no means
of identification on him other than his school cap and blazer and so it
was several hours before the parents were located by the police. Once the
parents knew Jack was going to live they moved house so that in future
he could walk to school and also installed a telephone for the first time
in their lives.

PARENTAL ATTITUDES

For several weeks Jack was unconscious; then he remained paralysed
and speechless for several more weeks; his skull had been badly dented
and he needed several operations and skin grafts on his face. Gradually
he began to recover and eventually even his educational attainments
returned. Then just when he was due to go back to school, he had an
epileptic seizure. He was put on drugs and his mother was told to take
great care of him. There had been no need to tell her to do so. In fact
the accident had changed her from a warmhearted, affectionate but
easy-going and somewhat indulgent mother into an overanxious, ever
watchful nagging hypochondriac. She could not bear to let Jack out of
her sight, insisted on taking and fetching him from school, would not
allow him out to play with other boys and overfed him in her anxiety
that he should get quite well. Thus his obesity was not so much a conse-
quence of his accident, as she thought, but resulted from lack of exercise and overeating.

The father had shared his wife's concern in the beginning but now
felt she was rather overdoing it. However, she became so overwrought
when he tried to support the boy's pleas to let him go out and play, that
he had given up in the hope in time she would get over it. Meanwhile,
Jack had grown increasingly unhappy, being practically confined either
to the parlour at home or to his classroom. His mother had impressed
upon the school that 'on doctor's orders he was not to be allowed into
the playground or the playing fields'. Though this was not strictly
speaking true she sincerely believed that she was interpreting the doctor's intention. Partly in reaction to this severely restricting, overpro-

tective regime and partly because Jack was growing depressed about having to some extent remained physically handicapped, he was becoming increasingly moody and given to sudden outbursts of temper, followed by bouts of weeping and contrition.

During one of his periodic visits to the hospital the surgeon commented how well Jack had recovered. To the doctor's surprise the mother burst into tears, crying 'you doctors have done miracles for his body but you have done nothing for his mind'. Thereupon he was referred to us for help.

SUMMARY AND RECOMMENDATIONS

It was impossible to tell whether Jack's personality had changed as a result of the accident and perhaps also the drugs he was now taking; or whether his depression, tearfulness, passivity and slowness were predominantly psychological reactions, partly due to delayed shock and partly due to his mother's grossly overprotective attitude. To give both of them a break, it was recommended that Jack be sent to a children's convalescent home and the hospital gave their full backing. Previously the mother had rejected a similar offer but now she was ready to give it a try as Jack's unhappiness was becoming unbearable to her.

SUBSEQUENT DEVELOPMENTS

During his two months away, he almost changed back into his pre-accident self. His mobility had been steadily improving anyhow, but being allowed to try ball games, climbing and other physical activities enabled him to make great strides forward. The persistence he had always shown now stood him in good stead as he was willing to go on practising movements and skills he had lost. Now, too, his previous personality began to emerge and he also lost some weight. On his return home, his parents were overjoyed: it seemed as if Jack had at last been fully restored to them. There was no need to reassure them that there had neither been a personality change nor a neurotic illness as this was now patently obvious.

Meanwhile the mother had been given help to understand and overcome her feelings of guilt and anxiety about Jack's accident. Once we knew from reports by the convalescent home how things were going, we also prepared her to face the need for a changed regime when he came back.

At school Jack's work was now improving also, but he continued to be rather slow. When he failed the special entrance examination to the Catholic grammar school (he just scraped through the city's 11-plus exam) a special case was made out jointly by the accident hospital and ourselves for making an exception of Jack because of the exceptional circumstances. There was every hope that he would completely recover, and once the drugs were discontinued there was a good chance that he might regain his former speed of work. Eventually the school agreed and Jack wrote his first poem in the form of a thanksgiving prayer to God, the hospital and me. Two years later he sent me a 'special painting to commemorate how you truly brought me back to a life worth living'.

PROGNOSIS

Though he never regained his former physical agility and prowess, he canalised his passion for sport into refereeing instead. Similarly, he learned to overcome or circumvent the few minor disabilities which remained. Holding his own in the grammar school never became easy but he expected no special concessions once he had been admitted. His courage, persistence and ingenuity in coping have won him the admirations and friendship of boys and masters alike. Now he is on the point of entering the sixth form. The pride of his family has been a great support to him and they have marvelled that he should have been the only one of their five children who gained admission to the grammar school.

PART 2

Facts and Figures
for the 103 Children

The statistical material which provides an overall picture of the children and their background is presented in this section but the detailed tables have been placed at the end of the book to preserve contextual continuity (pages 145 to 158).

6. How the Children Came to be Examined

As part of its research programme the Department of Child Study in the university where this study was carried out, undertook a long-term investigation of the conditions associated with learning difficulties in children of average or above intelligence. Learning ability was interpreted in a wide sense: it included pupils whose educational attainments were considered unsatisfactory in one or more respects as well as those whose behaviour was considered unsatisfactory, i.e. their social or emotional learning was inadequate.

Whoever actually requested that a child be given a psychological examination in the department, the same procedure was adopted in every case. The school was asked to make a report on a standard assessment schedule designed to give a picture of the child's educational attainment, other abilities and behaviour in the classroom and with other children. In cases where the child had recently been receiving medical treatment for a condition possibly associated with his present learning difficulties, a medical report was also obtained.

Then the parents were invited to bring the child to the department for a detailed psychological examination which included a battery of intelligence, attainment and personality assessments; opportunity was also provided for observing his behaviour in more unstructured situations, such as playing by himself and with other children, using a punch ball, climbing apparatus, paint, clay, etc. Meanwhile, the parents were interviewed by a psychiatric social worker to obtain information on the home background, parental attitudes to the child, his school and his educational progress. The minimum time given to interviewing each child and the parents was three hours; but on several occasions it proved necessary to arrange a second session to obtain further information or to have the opportunity for further observation when the child might feel more at ease after having made the initial contact.

Subsequently, a case conference was held to bring together all the findings. Usually the headteacher or whoever made the initial referral was invited to join this discussion. At the case conference hypotheses were formulated to account for the child's difficulties and to consider possible recommendations which might improve, or better still, resolve the situation. Then another interview was arranged with the parents to discuss with them our conclusions and recommendations. Finally a detailed, written report was sent to the referring agency which also indicated whether or not the parents were prepared to accept whatever recommendations had been made.

The group of children who are the subjects of this study were referred to the department between 1956 to 1961. Subsequently from all the cases referred to the department during this five-year period, all those whose intelligence quotients were found to be 120 and above were made the subjects of this study. All our usual procedures, adopted for psychological assessment, had been followed and at the time of seeing the children it had not been decided to make this study. Later, their case files were used for extracting all the available information which was in every case recorded in a standard way just as the broad lines of the investigation itself always followed a standard pattern to ensure comparability.

During the period in question, altogether 468 children were examined. Of these 103 or some 23 per cent were found to have intelligence quotients of 120 or above. In a large unselected population about 11 per cent would be expected to have superior quotients of this order (Bernreuter, 1938), but of course children referred to a university department's teaching and demonstration centre are inevitably even more highly selected. All that can be said is that they are probably typical of very able children who have educational or behaviour difficulties sufficiently serious to lead teachers or parents to seek special help. Of the 103 children, seventy-five were boys and twenty-eight girls. Thus among this highly selected group, boys outnumber girls in the ratio of about three to one in the same way as is found generally with regard to educational and adjustment difficulties. Their ages ranged from four and a half to eighteen years, the average being ten and a half years. The majority of referrals were made by headteachers, the others by professional agencies of various kinds and by parents themselves (Table 1). About a third of the children were attending secondary schools while the majority were still at primary school; a small minority went to private as against state schools (Table 2). The reason for referral was, in the great majority of cases, some form of educational difficulty, while behaviour problems were present in over a third of the group; in about a fifth of the sample both types of problem were reported. Hence there are more reasons than the total number of children (Table 3). Only a small number had physical disabilities.

The actual subject in which the child was doing badly is shown in Table 4. More than half of those referred for educational difficulties only, were reported to be doing badly in all their school work. The proportion of children who had difficulties respectively in arithmetic, reading or spelling was roughly similar, namely about 20 per cent in each of these subjects. The number of those who had 'other difficulties' with school work, such as refusing to do homework, working only when compelled or closely supervised, was also in the region of 20 per cent; in this respect boys outnumbered girls by three to one. The proportion of boys who had reading difficulties was also larger than girls, while the position was reversed with regard to spelling.

7. The Characteristics of Able Misfits

Intelligence and attainments

At the time of the first examination, the average age of the children was ten and a half years. Boys tended to be referred rather younger than girls (by some eighteen months). On the one hand, the girls spanned a wider age range (from four and a half to eighteen years); the boys, on the other hand, showed a considerably wider I.Q. range and the two highest intelligence quotients (208 and the next highest of 181) were both scored by boys. However, there was little difference in the average intelligence level of boys and girls respectively, which was around the 130 mark. This is generally considered to be 'good honours degree standard'. The majority, some 78 per cent, had I.Q.s between 120 and 139 (Tables 5, 6 and 7).

Several of the children were referred primarily for behaviour rather than educational difficulties; even in some of the latter cases, standardised tests were either inappropriate or their ceiling was not high enough for the ablest or oldest in this group. This is illustrated by the case of a fourteen-year-old boy with an I.Q. of 168; he attended a grammar school and was reported to be a 'mathematical genius' and 'pretty outstanding at most other subjects' but quite unwilling to do any homework.

Hence educational test results are available for only a proportion of the total sample (Tables 8, 9 and 10). The seventy-seven children who were given a reading test did little better on average than the majority of pupils of their own age, despite their very good intellectual ability. This was equally true of boys and girls. The position was very similar with regard to arithmetic while in spelling they were even worse, both sexes receiving a score one year below their chronological age. It goes, of course, without saying that in all three subjects the children's attainments were several years below their mental age level. Neither I.Q. levels nor ranges are shown again, since in every case they varied little from those obtained by the whole group of children (Table 5).

To explore in greater detail the extent of educational difficulties, attainment levels in the various subjects were compared both with chronological and mental ages. Between a quarter to a half of the children obtained scores which were one or two years below their actual age; and the number whose scores were two years or more below their chronological age was still sizeable (some 25 per cent), except for arithmetic. Thus there was a considerable degree of educational backwardness. This was somewhat unexpected since one would assume that very intelligent children would at least be able to reach the average scholastic standard attained by the majority of their contemporaries.

When comparisons were made between educational and mental age levels, the standard of the great majority was found to be two or more years below their own mental capacity. Thus the extent and degree of underfunctioning or underachievement was very considerable (Table 11).

The report form, which schools were requested to complete, asked for information on each child's ability and attainment. For attainment the assessments corresponded extremely closely to the test results obtained during the psychological interview. This stands in marked contrast with the schools' assessment of intelligence: less than half of the group of 103 children were judged to be of good or very good ability, the majority being thought of as average or even below average in intelligence. Such a serious underestimate suggests that teachers judge intelligence primarily by a pupil's level of educational achievement.

There is evidence from other studies to show that children live up (or down) to their teacher's expectations; as long as their ability remains unrecognised, underfunctioning but able children are unlikely to receive the necessary encouragement from their teachers to reach the much higher level of attainment of which they are capable. Moreover, since most teachers aim at the average of their form and since most of our sample were not in the top stream, the chances of the children being sufficiently stretched and stimulated were also rather slim.

For some fifty-two children, the school supplied the results of various group intelligence tests. In every case, whatever test was used, the results were below those the child achieved during the individual interview. While the group test quotients ranged from 115 to 135, the individual intelligence test quotients ranged from 125 to 150. These findings reflect the fact that underfunctioning and maladjusted children usually fail to do themselves justice in group tests, partly because of their resemblance to scholastic tests and partly because of the absence of encouragement and praise which form an integral part of individual test procedures.

Emotional adjustment

Information was obtained from three sources: the report given by the school; the interview with the parents; and the psychological assessment of the child himself. Only 20 per cent of all the children showed no symptom of emotional disturbance, either at home or at school. A similar proportion, 18 per cent, had primarily behaviour problems, while the majority had educational difficulties, accompanied by more or less serious emotional problems. This suggests that the interrelationship between these two aspects of growth is as close among very able as it is among ordinary children. In most cases, symptoms of maladjustment were shown both at home and at school (Table 12).

These symptoms were classified in two different ways (Tables 13 to 16). First, five descriptive categories were used according to the predominant, manifest behaviour patterns exhibited by the child: normal, anxious, withdrawn, aggressive and 'mixed' behaviour. 'Normal' meant that either no symptom was shown or at most two, none of which were likely to indicate serious maladjustment; for example daydreaming, sibling jealousy, lack of concentration or nailbiting. A child was classified as 'anxious' when he was reported to be highly strung, tense, lacking in confidence and overtimid. Those said to be unresponsive, solitary, living in a world of their own and never to approach spontaneously their teachers or classmates, were described as being 'withdrawn'. The child who showed frequent temper outbursts or destructive, unmanageable, insolent behaviour was classified as 'aggressive', and lastly, a 'mixed' pattern was characterised by a combination of withdrawn, aggressive or anxious behaviour.

Among the whole group of able children, anxious and withdrawn behaviour predominated. However, there was a marked sex difference: half the girls had symptoms of anxiety while none showed 'mixed' behaviour. Among the boys, no one behaviour pattern predominated but some 25 per cent showed 'mixed' behaviour. There was also a sex difference both in the number of symptoms (mean for boys 4·2 and for girls 3·1) and in the greater proportion of boys showing five or more symptoms (45 per cent as against only 18 per cent of girls). On average anxious children exhibited the least and the 'mixed' group the greatest number of symptoms.

Secondly symptoms of maladjustment were grouped under the three main categories used by the Underwood Committee (1955), namely nervous, habit and behaviour disorders. Using this system of classification, boys were again found to show a greater number of symptoms. For both sexes, habit disorders were least frequent and nervous symptoms most common. The most frequent single symptom was lack of confidence, both among the whole group and among each of the sexes. Next in order of frequency were lack of concentration and solitariness among boys, whereas among girls being highly strung and overtimid ranked next. While a higher proportion of boys were reported to show symptoms of aggression, a higher proportion of girls were said to be insolent or unmanageable.

There was a marked difference between the sexes in the incidence of restlessness, unresponsiveness, speech difficulty, asthma, sibling jealousy and stealing, boys showing a much higher incidence in every case. Certain symptoms were completely absent among girls, such as restlessness, food fads, wetting, soiling and asthma; the least frequent symptoms among boys were also food fads, wetting and soiling. Fewer boys than girls had sleep disturbances.

Exploring the relation between predominant behaviour patterns and symptoms of maladjustment (arranged according to the Underwood classification), nervous symptoms were found to predominate among withdrawn children and behaviour disorders among aggressive ones; habit disorders were most frequent among the 'mixed' group. Of course, the three symptom categories were not mutually exclusive; for example, among the anxious children two-thirds showed nervous symptoms, 10 per cent habit disorders and 21 per cent behaviour difficulties.

The incidence of lefthandedness was 8 per cent among boys which is identical with the national figure. None of the girls were found to be left-handed as compared with some 6 per cent among girls in general.

Social competence

To assess this aspect of development, the Vineland Social Maturity Scale was administered. As this test becomes less discriminating above the ten year level, it was given only to those below this age, some fifty children in all. On average their level of social competence was eight months below their chronological age and only three children scored a social age a year above their actual age. All the children showed a marked discrepancy between their mental and social age; this amounted to four years or more in half the group (Table 17).

One would not, of course, expect very able children to be as advanced socially as they are intellectually (Pringle, 1966); but it does seem a sign of social immaturity not to have reached at least the level of their own chronological age. These results confirm the information obtained by the social worker that the parents were reluctant to grant and to foster their children's independence (Chapter 8, p. 81).

Educational difficulties and emotional adjustment

The relationship between the number of symptoms shown by each child
—irrespective of type or severity—and the school subject in which he
was retarded (by two years or more compared with his mental age) was
explored. For this purpose, the total sample was divided into two groups,
those showing none, one or two symptoms only, and those showing
three or more symptoms. About half the number of children fell into
each of these two groups; the average age and intelligence quotient
were very similar in each and so comparable to those of the whole group.
However, the proportion of boys to girls was much higher among those
with many symptoms, there being nearly four times as many boys. The
proportion of retarded children was higher among those with many
symptoms in relation to every school subject.

Lastly, a comparison was made between children whose reading level
was two years or more above their attainment in arithmetic and those
where the position of these subjects was reversed. As numbers in each
group were very small, the trends which emerged can only be considered
as being suggestive. Those whose reading was better, showed nearly
twice as many symptoms; they also differed from the 'better' arithmeti-
cian in being more solitary, withdrawn and given to daydreaming.
Among both groups, nervous symptoms predominated (Tables 18
and 19).

Summary

What does the 'average able misfit' of our study look like? It is three
times as likely that he will be a boy, aged ten and a half years and thus
nearing the end of his junior school career. In all these respects he
closely resembles all children referred for educational or psychological
help.

Despite good intelligence, his reading and arithmetic are only just
average for his age and spelling is even weaker. Probably because of
this undistinguished scholastic record, his teacher is as likely as not to
consider him to be only an averagely able pupil. In this she would be
further confirmed by the results of group intelligence tests, since he is
unlikely to do himself justice in them.

It is highly likely that he will show some symptoms of emotional
difficulties; these will be more serious as well as more numerous if he
is a boy. His social competence will be, at best, only average for his age.

8. Home Background and Parental Attitudes

Socio-economic factors

The level of paternal occupational status was considerably higher than would be expected in a random sample; over 70 per cent belonged to professional and other non-manual occupations, which is about twice as many as in the population as a whole (Table 20). Similarly a high proportion among both parents went to grammar or selective secondary schools and 25 per cent had either professional training or a university education (Table 21). At the time of the child's examination, about a third of the mothers were working, either part- or full-time. The majority were living in a house which they owned or were in the process of buying, though as many as one in five families were sharing accommodation with relatives (Table 22).

Family structure

The majority of children (62 per cent) were firstborn which is a much higher proportion than in the ordinary population (Table 23). For example, in McLaren's Scottish Survey (1950) there were 39 per cent and in the more recent National Child Development Study (1958 Cohort) the incidence was 38 per cent (Pringle, Butler and Davie, 1966). The incidence of an only child was one in four and those occupying a middle position in the family were the smallest group by far (10 per cent). A rather similar picture emerged when the position in the family was analysed for those children referred mainly because of behaviour difficulties. In their case, the proportion of firstborn was even higher (some 71 per cent) while those occupying a middle position comprised a very small group indeed (Table 24).

One can but speculate on the significance of these facts: are parents more ambitious or anxious for their firstborn? Are they less sensible or relaxed, because inexperienced, in their handling? Is being the oldest or only child an emotionally more intense and thus vulnerable position? Do very intelligent children find this a particularly difficult situation?

79

These questions deserve further exploration, particularly since other studies of children with learning or adjustment difficulties have not reported a predominance of children occupying this position in the family.

A comparison was also made between firstborn children and the rest with regard to the predominant behaviour pattern shown by them (Table 25). While anxiety was less frequent among firstborn, the incidence of both withdrawn and aggressive behaviour was higher among them than those occupying other positions in the family. Does this reflect the fact that the firstborn, when eventually faced with a competitor (unless he remains an only child), is likely to react either by trying to assert his dominance over his potential rival or else refuses to compete and withdraws into himself; whereas those who occupy other positions in the family, have had to live with a rival right from the start and hence tend to be more anxious about 'making out'?

Next, the incidence of atypical family situations was explored. All such situations were included, from children living with only one parent because of desertion, divorce, separation, death or illegitimacy; to those with one step-parent as well as children who were adopted. A considerably greater number than among the population at large were not living with both their own mother and father (18 per cent as against 6 per cent found in the national survey by Pringle, Butler and Davie, 1966).

Cultural and social opportunities

The assessment of cultural opportunities available in the home was based on the number and types of daily papers taken; the books read; the type of radio and TV programme regularly enjoyed by the family; and the kind of outings and visits arranged by the parents to broaden the children's experience and background. A three point scale was used, average, below and above average. In her interview the psychiatric social worker obtained as much detailed factual information as possible, which was then rated by her as well as by three other staff members independently. Agreement proved to be high. Cases where ratings differed were discussed to arrive at an agreed solution. The yardstick for making these ratings was the staff's wide professional knowledge and experience of all types and levels of homes.

Despite the high socio-economic status of our able misfits, only about a third of the homes were judged to provide an above average level of cultural stimulation. Examining the same aspect in relation to the fathers' occupational status, differences between the social groups were in the expected direction: just over half the professional/managerial homes provided above average stimulation, while none of the skilled/

unskilled homes did so; non-manual homes occupied a position midway. Conversely, in the majority of skilled/unskilled homes there was a below average level of cultural stimulation but it is even more noteworthy that this was also the case in a sizeable minority of professional/managerial homes (21 per cent). Thus the overall picture indicated a less satisfactory situation than one would have expected from the socio-economic standing of the families. It accords, however, with findings from other studies (Zweig, 1961).

For judging the children's leisure interests and occupations, the main criteria were their strength and persistence. Again, these were assessed on a three-point scale in the same way as described above. Contrary to what one would have expected, in view of the children's good ability, less than one in five were rated as having above average interests and hobbies while almost half of them fell below average. Nor were those from professional/managerial homes very markedly superior to those from the other two occupational groups (Tables 24 and 26).

Next, opportunities given to the children for gaining independence were explored. Here such questions were looked at as whether parents encouraged them to be responsible for their own personal care, expected them to help at home with chores such as bedmaking or shoe cleaning, allowed them to go about the neighbourhood unaccompanied, do some shopping and spend their own pocket money. The same three point rating scale of average, below and above average was used.

Few children seemed to be given above average opportunities while for about half of them these were less than average. More boys than girls had above average opportunities and of the three occupational groups the non-manual one granted the most independence.

Last, opportunities available to the children for social contact with contemporaries were considered. Informal opportunities, such as playing in gardens, streets, at home and in other children's houses, as well as more formal, organised activities, such as scouts and clubs, were included. The periods before and after starting school were considered separately. During the pre-school stage, the majority of boys and girls had had rather limited social contacts. Even when they began to attend school, more than half of them still had below average opportunities for social experiences with their contemporaries.

The overall proportion of children who enjoyed above average opportunities, was very small and virtually the same before and after going to school; however, there was a sex difference, since no girl had above average opportunity during the pre-school stage but subsequently a small proportion did so. The picture was different for those children who had had below average opportunities to mix with others before

4

starting school: their proportion dropped from two-thirds to about half, once they began attending school.

Looking at opportunities for social contact in relation to occupational grouping, children from professional/managerial homes were found to be particularly restricted, both before and after starting school. The majority of children from the other two occupational groupings had average or above average opportunities available. The non-manual group fared best of all in this respect (Tables 28 and 29).

There are a number of possible explanations for the apparently limited social contact with contemporaries, available to our group of children. The simplest is that opportunities were curtailed by the area in which the family lived, i.e. that there were few other children nearby. However, this is unlikely to account for more than a minority of cases. Alternatively, the parents may not have wanted such contact for their children or at least did not go out of their way to encourage it. Another possibility is that the children themselves did not find congenial companions either in the neighbourhood or at school; this may have been particularly so for the ablest of them.

Home atmosphere

This was assessed on a three point scale, harmonious, fair and unfavourable. In the first group were placed those families which seemed to be normally happy, closely knit yet without undue possessiveness, and not disrupted by rivalries or other dissatisfactions. Those families in which there seemed to be relatively minor signs of strain were placed in the second group; this included some quarrelling, interference from relatives and unsatisfactory sexual relationships. The last category was applied to all homes where there was a serious and prolonged degree of strain and tension.

Altogether, the atmosphere of 46 per cent of the homes was judged to be unfavourable and of 13 per cent fair; the remainder (41 per cent) seemed to be harmonious. Causes ranged from severe financial difficulties to chronic parental disharmony. In a proportion of families (some 18 per cent) this was due not merely to temperamental incompatibility but to emotional instability on the part of one or both partners, or a relative living with them. A minority had to be regarded as 'broken homes' (some 9 per cent), even though in some cases this was so in spirit but not yet actually in fact.

The predominant behaviour pattern shown by the children was analysed in relation to the home atmosphere. As expected, harmonious homes had by far the highest proportion of children whose behaviour was judged to be normal for their age; none showed mixed behaviour and only a small minority were anxious, aggressive or withdrawn. Conversely, where there was a serious degree of tension and strain in the home, only a very small proportion of children showed no behaviour difficulties whatever. The great majority (92 per cent) showed one type of disturbance or another, the single highest group being anxious children. A fairly similar but less severe pattern of disturbance characterised children from homes where there was some degree of strain (Table 30).

Discipline

The methods of discipline used by parents were classified into four groups: sensible, strict, indulgent and inconsistent. By sensible was meant a balanced approach, appropriate to the child's age and understanding. Inconsistency could show itself in two different ways: one or both parents might be inconsistent in the use of praise and punishment; or the inconsistency might lie in the fact that the parents disagreed on methods of discipline, even though each consistently applied his chosen approach.

More than a third of the children (37 per cent) were subjected to inconsistent handling and this was more marked for boys than girls. Discipline was sensible in about one case in four and there was little difference between the sexes. About the same proportion of children were overindulged, boys rather more frequently than girls. Strict discipline was only used to a limited extent (13 per cent) but rather unexpectedly was more frequently applied to girls than to boys (25 per cent as against 9 per cent). Analysing methods of discipline in relations to paternal occupational status showed that professional and managerial homes had the highest incidence of inconsistency; the middle occupational range contained the highest proportion of parents applying sensible handling; and in skilled and unskilled homes the highest incidence of indulgence was found (Tables 31 and 32).

Methods of parental discipline were then examined in relation to the predominant behaviour pattern shown by the children. As expected, a majority had no behaviour difficulties where parental handling was judged to be sensible. Strict discipline resulted in a polarisation of behaviour, nearly half the children being anxious and one in four aggressive; none showed mixed behaviour, possibly an indication that at least children know where they are under such a regime. Parental indulgence also led to polarised behaviour, this time being expressed in either withdrawn or mixed responses; this suggests that the overindulged child may opt for passivity when he is not given similar consideration by others or else will vascillate between aggressive resentment and withdrawal. The lowest incidence of normal adjustment was found among children subjected to inconsistent discipline. Among them, a high proportion (more than one in three) showed mixed behaviour; this probably reflects the fact that inconsistent handling provokes uncertainty and hence fluctuation in responding to adults (Table 33).

Parental attitudes to child's educational progress and emotional development

These were rated along a four point scale, ranging from normal interest and concern to an overanxious attitude or indifference. The majority of parents showed either normal interest or concern, but over a third were inclined to be overanxious concerning their child's educational progress. An insignificant minority (2 per cent) were indifferent about it. There was relatively little difference in attitude towards boys and girls respectively.

There was less parental concern or overanxiety about the child's emotional development which was to be expected since only a minority were showing serious behaviour difficulties. However, an unexpectedly high proportion, more than one in four parents, were indifferent about this aspect of growth. Again, attitudes towards boys and girls did not differ materially (Tables 34 and 35).

When parental attitudes towards educational progress were considered in relation to the fathers' occupational status, the differences emerged were in the expected direction: in the professional/managerial group, more than half were overanxious and a further third were concerned, while none were indifferent; similarly, in the non-manual group none of the parents were indifferent to their child's educational progress, but a considerably smaller proportion (some 15 per cent) were overanxious. Both in this group and in the skilled/unskilled group about a third of the parents took a normal interest but in the latter group a minority (11 per cent) were indifferent.

There was far less difference between the three occupational groups in their attitude to the child's emotional development than there had been regarding educational progress. Overall, a much greater proportion were indifferent, as many as a third in the lowest occupational group, but even among professional/managerial parents a quarter felt this way. The non-manual group were the least overanxious (11 per cent) whereas in the two other categories about one in four or five parents (skilled/unskilled and professional/managerial respectively) took this attitude. Normal interest was expressed by about a third in the top two groups and by a fifth of the lowest group (Tables 36 and 37).

Summary

What then characterised the home background and the parental attitudes of our 'able misfits'? Their parents were well educated and the majority were professional or non-manual workers. Firstborn children predominated. The incidence of atypical family situations was higher than in the population at large but this may well apply generally to children referred for psychological help. Rather less than half the homes were judged to have a happy and harmonious atmosphere. Somewhat unexpected was the finding that above average cultural and social opportunities were provided by only a minority of parents; this applied also to the provision of leisure activities.

Parental discipline seemed sensible in only one case out of four and inconsistent handling was most prominent in professional class homes. The child's educational progress was of concern to almost all parents which contrasted with parental attitudes regarding the child's emotional development; this appeared to be of little importance to a sizeable minority.

Are these homes typical in any way of those in which 'able misfits' grow up? To what extent do they contribute or possibly cause the child's educational and behaviour difficulties? Or, put the other way round, do very intelligent children have special needs which tend to be met only exceptionally and which make them particularly vulnerable to the stresses of ordinary family life? None of these questions can be answered with certainty. However, the lack of a harmonious and stimulating home background impedes the optimal development of any child's potentialities. Our findings suggest that good intellectual ability by itself is insufficient to compensate for inadequate parental support and interest.

9. Recommendations Made and Subsequent Developments

Recommendations made

For every child all the relevant information was brought together at a case conference to decide what action ought to be taken. More than one recommendation was made in some cases. The most frequent single suggestion was attendance at the department for remedial work and play therapy.

Next in order of frequency came advice, either to the parents or the school, or to both. There were a number of possible reasons why only advice was given. At best, it was felt this was all that was needed and that it would be acted upon. In cases where the child attended boarding school or where the family lived a long way away, regular attendance at the department was impossible for practical reasons. If treatment was thought to be desirable, the advice given would include referral to a geographically more accessible service. At worst, the parents were refusing to accept the diagnosis and the offer of psychological help; thus only advice would be given coupled with the suggestion that if they changed their mind, the matter could be reopened. Fortunately such outright rejection was relatively rare.

There were also some more specific recommendations, such as that the child should be moved to another stream or to another school altogether; or that a specialist medical examination be carried out; or that the child be recalled for a re-examination in the department within a six to twelve month period. In a small proportion of cases private tuition was suggested (Table 38).

Subsequent development

Attendance was recommended for sixty-five children, forty-seven boys and eighteen girls. In three cases the parents changed their mind and refused treatment when a vacancy was offered to them. Of the remaining sixty-two children, some fourteen were in the first place to come for a period of observation lasting no longer than a term, when the situation would be reviewed. Attendance meant in every case a weekly visit of about two hours' duration.

Of the forty-eight children who were given remedial treatment and play therapy, twenty-five attended for six months, twenty for up to a year and three for longer than that. Three years after the last child had ceased attending, contact was made with the parents to enquire how the child was now getting on. Where possible, a personal visit was paid while in the rest of the cases a follow-up letter was sent. Information was obtained on forty children, i.e. some 83 per cent. Of these, four were still pupils at the boarding schools to which they had been admitted on our recommendation, subsequent to receiving weekly treatment. Two of them were reported to be making excellent progress, one good progress, and another had remained emotionally disturbed and educationally backward though he was said to be improving very slowly.

Of the thirty-six children living at home and attending day schools, the majority (twenty-two) were no longer causing concern to their parents; eight children were said to be still 'not doing as well as they could in school'; four were reported to show both learning and behaviour difficulties though neither were as severe as they had previously been; and two children were 'difficult to manage at home' though not at school where both their progress and behaviour were reported to be satisfactory. One of them was adopted and the other had acquired a stepmother, his father having obtained a divorce from the child's mother.

A report was also obtained from the schools of the forty children whose parents responded to the follow-up enquiry. Though it was favourable in the majority of cases (thirty children), this is less satisfactory than appears since ten of them were attending secondary modern or private schools, having failed the 11-plus selective examination. For another ten children the school's report indicated that there was still a serious degree of underfunctioning. However, behaviour difficulties were reported for two children only. The teachers were in every case aware of the child's good intellectual level, probably because the parents had communicated this fact or because our report had been passed on; otherwise a different picture might well have emerged, since in half the cases educational attainments were merely good average in relation to chronological age.

Though a follow-up was attempted only for those children who had had a regular period of treatment, all parents had been told to get in touch with us again should they or the school grow once more concerned about the child's progress or adjustment. That none of them did so cannot, of course, be taken as an indication that none felt such concern.

In some cases, too, parents or school may have felt that the first intervention had not achieved enough and they would therefore be disinclined
to seek help again. However, since at the time of the initial interview a
considerable proportion of parents seemed overanxious about their
child (Tables 34 and 35), it is perhaps a reasonable inference either that
things had improved or that parental attitudes had become modified.
And since we remained in touch with many of the schools over other
children, reopening a particular case would have been an easy matter.

Conclusions

Two outstanding features emerge from this study of very intelligent
children: first, that in the great majority of cases learning difficulties
were accompanied, or found in association with, emotional or behaviour problems; secondly, that these were associated with a multiplicity
of factors, rather than one or two major causes. Hence it looks as if the
learning and adjustment problems of the very able are, in essence, very
similar to those of children in general.

PART 3

The Psychology of Learning and Adjustment

This section presents a more theoretical discussion of children's basic psychological needs, the link between learning and emotion, and the meaning and interpretation of symptoms of emotional adjustment. Then the research literature on able misfits is briefly reviewed.

10. Learning and Emotion

Searching for the relationship

It is now becoming increasingly recognised that enquiring about the relationship between learning and emotion is to pose an almost meaningless question. The study of how children learn was for a long time considered mainly in the narrow context of scholastic achievement; and, consequently, during the past forty years much time and effort was devoted to attempts at measurement, particularly in the fields of general intelligence and educational attainments. Though learning theories were subsequently placed into a wider framework, those psychologists interested primarily in personality development and human motivation doubted the relevance of simple schemes of rewards and punishment to human motivation, even if appropriate to that of animals. Paradoxically enough it is recent work with animals which has conferred or rather restored academic respectability to the study of emotion.

Its study has also had a rather chequered career. At the turn of the century it was held that the behaviour of animals should not be explained in terms of human attributes if it could be explained on a lower level. Fifty years later this was subtly inverted: many psychologists had become reluctant to attribute to humans any characteristics which could not be observed, or better still measured, in lower animals. Moreover, emotion came to be regarded in psychological writing primarily as a form of disorder or distress. The simple notion that it is involved in the whole business of living had somehow been lost sight of.

Practising psychologists, whether of a psychoanalytical, eclectically dynamic or developmental persuasion, had, of course, continued to take emotion into account since their everyday work made it impossible to ignore its all-pervasive influence. Reinstatement, however, stems from the work of ecologists who showed that monkeys, dogs and even rats learned better and grew into more effective adult animals if their emotional needs had been satisfied early in life. And so it has come about that writers, holding different theoretical viewpoints, now consider the

need for affection either equal or next in importance to the basic
physical needs. Searching for the relationship between learning and
emotion has been replaced by a study of their earliest appearance and
form.

Learning to learn

It all starts very early. So early that, like the proverbial chicken and egg
question, it is fruitless to ask which comes first, learning or emotion. A
baby begins to learn from the day he is born and from this day too, he is
affected by parental, particularly maternal love. At best such love is
unconditional: he is valued for his own sake and not because he is a boy
or girl, fair or dark, beautiful or plain. This caring affection is so all-
pervasive that it communicates itself to him in everything his mother
does for him.

Through being loved, the baby learns to feel love for her and goes
on to learn what is involved in making a relationship with another
person: that it implies not only receiving but also giving affection; not
only making demands but being willing to satisfy the demands of others;
no longer expecting immediate satisfaction but being willing to accept
the frustration of delay; and being prepared to subordinate one's wishes
to those of others instead of being completely self-centred. Because of
this reciprocal bond he perseveres with learning to be dry and clean, to
walk, to talk and eventually to succeed with school learning. If this early
experience of love has been lacking, if he has been rejected or deprived,
his learning will remain slow, difficult and often inadequate. According
to his temperament, he will either be apathetic or unresponsive, or he
will fight and protest against every new demand which is made upon
him. He will have failed to learn three basic lessons: a pleasurable
awareness of his own identity, his self; the joy of a mutually rewarding
relationship; and a desire for approval, which acts as a spur to
learning.

The self has been defined as 'reflected appraisals' which implies that
whether a child develops a constructive or destructive attitude to himself,
and subsequently to other people, depends in the first place on his
parents' attitude to him. The more cherished he is, the more he comes
to feel himself to be a worthwhile person. Similarly, being loved, he
learns to give love and trust. Thirdly, and perhaps most important for
the achievement of his potential, the pleasure of his parents in his progress provides the main incentive for his learning. For example, the
mother who thinks her baby has said his first word, does in fact, almost
unintentionally, accelerate his actually doing so. Because she shows
pleasure at sounds which resemble words, he will make these sounds

more often, thus practising those that evoke her smiles and nods. Her approval, and later that of other adults important to him, is the main incentive, the chief motivating force which makes him want to conform to her expectations and demands.

Conversely, the infant soon learns that his failure to co-operate in say, toilet training, evokes his mother's displeasure which is a painful and anxiety-provoking experience; painful because it deprives him of the satisfying feeling of her approval and anxiety-provoking because it contains the threat of losing her love. Even very young infants sense their mother's displeasure or disturbed emotional tone, and react by becoming restless, irritable, difficult over feeding and so on.

It can be argued that the more love a child is given, the more readily will he become anxious when he encounters the threat of losing it, even temporarily. Such a theory accounts for the apparent paradox that in a rejecting home or in an institution a child is less anxious about successful learning than if he grows up in the warm, accepting atmosphere of a happy family. The reason is that the greater the sense of love and acceptance, the more distinctive are the cues of disapproval, of loss of love. More distinctive, unequivocal cues make learning easier. This view of learning and emotion also supports a common clinical finding: it is the overprotected child who is the most anxious; for the rejected and deprived the cues tend to be blurred. A similar blurring may be caused by inconsistent handling which confuses the child and interferes with his learning to distinguish between acceptable and unacceptable behaviour.

During growth from infancy to childhood both desire for approval and anxiety in the face of disapproval continue to play an important part. Anxiety is such a painful and disturbing emotion that most children will go to considerable lengths to avoid behaviour that is likely to arouse it. Because he wishes to avoid this feeling, he learns to be considerate in his relations with others and to conform to customs and taboos. Conversely, approval is so pleasurable that the parent, by his very interest, makes learning new skills an enjoyable activity. His encouragement and recognition of the child's effort to master his environment is not only the most potent motivating force; it will also determine his later attitudes to the more formal learning demanded of him in school. For some time to come, parents and teachers will play a powerful role in fostering the desire to go on learning; though with increasing maturity the joy of new achievements becomes itself an increasingly powerful incentive. Whether the approval of one's peers ever becomes a negligible factor and whether learning for its own sake can become a sufficient motivation for the majority of children, remains open to doubt.

Be this as it may, emotion and learning are so closely interwoven from the earliest years that, rather than searching for links, they should be viewed as two sides of the same coin. And for the same reason, emotional difficulties more often than not affect educational progress, just as scholastic problems rarely continue for long without some emotional concomitants. Because relationships with significant adults, and later with the peer group, provide both the incentive and the conditions for learning, maladjustment and educational failure often follow similar paths. The affectionate and caring mother provides opportunities for satisfying her child's basic psychological needs; when one or more of these needs are not met, difficulties almost invariably arise. Even adults are prone to develop unfavourable reactions of various kinds if they remain unsatisfied for any length of time. For children, the satisfaction of these basic needs is of vital importance.

The basic psychological needs

Different schools of psychology offer a different list, ranging from as many as sixty to as few as two such needs. For most practical purposes, a fourfold classification seems to be sufficiently comprehensive. It covers the need for love and security; the need for new experiences; the need for achievement and recognition; and the need for responsibility and independence. Of course, they are closely interrelated and the growth of emotional resilience and intellectual development depends upon their satisfaction from birth to adolescence. They are listed in order of their relative importance during childhood: affection and security are the most essential needs of infancy while the other three needs become increasingly important as the child gets older.

These needs are also important in relation to motivation for school learning. This depends as much, if not more, on the pupil's willingness to learn as on his intelligence, the teacher's skill and the methods and materials which are used. Highly intelligent children, who yet do badly at school, clearly demonstrate this fact though it is equally true of the less able. While there are many ways in which scholastic progress can be fostered, the basis of stable and enduring motivation lies in the satisfaction of these four psychological needs.

The need for love and security

During the long and difficult business of growing up this is the most important need. The sense of being cherished whatever he may be like and whatever he may do, conveys this unconditional parental love. It is communicated to the child long before there is any conscious understanding or speech. Again, later at school the child will feel secure and wanted, if he is able to establish a satisfactory relationship with his teacher and feels able to win her approval. Both experience and research have shown the vital importance of receiving and giving affection; conversely, the lack of a close, continuous relationship with the mother, or a mother-substitute, especially in early childhood, impairs the child's capacity to make relationships subsequently.

A sense of security is acquired by a stable home background: parents whose attitudes and behaviour are consistent and predictable; a familiar place in which to live and play; a known and forseeable routine. The younger the child, the greater his need for security. Because one cannot readily give verbal explanations and reassurances to the infant or toddler, a change—be it of people, routine or total environment—is made more traumatic by its unexpectedness and apparent inexplicability. The child's need for and indeed craving for predictability is demonstrated by, for example, his insistence on having stories told in exactly the same words, whoever the teller.

Acceptance by contemporaries becomes of increasing importance as the middle years of childhood are reached. During adolescence the peer group will often exert a rival, if not more potent, influence than the family from which emancipation must eventually be achieved, until love and security are provided by the new family which the young adult has created for himself.

The need for new experiences

Just as physical growth depends on an adequate and balanced diet, so new experiences are the mental food required for intellectual growth. For the small baby everything is a new experience, from discovering his own body to observing the world around him. All normal children have a strong urge to explore, welcoming the challenge of new situations and gaining a sense of achievement from eventual mastery. The ability to move his limbs at will, to examine the texture, taste and smell of things, to crawl, walk and climb are new experiences in themselves, in addition to opening up an increasingly expanding environment for first-hand exploration; learning to understand speech and to talk himself promotes a vast new range of enquiry in which play and creative activities of all kinds have an important role.

At each developmental level from birth to maturity, tasks appropriate to the particular stage of growth are presented to the child and their mastery provides in turn the stepping-stone towards more difficult achievements. If denied the opportunity of appropriate experiences, no learning takes place; for example, in a non-speaking environment, the child will not learn to speak even though his hearing and speech apparatus are perfectly normal. The capacity to respond to education—in the widest sense of the word—depends as much on environmental opportunity and stimulation as it does on inborn capacity or ability to learn. Thus the emotional and cultural climate of the family, parental interest and ambition, standards of expected achievement both at home and at school, can foster or limit, and even seriously impair, intellectual development.

The need for achievement and recognition

Though mastering new skills and experiences is exciting, at the same time it inevitably brings some frustration or failure. If despite them the child is to continue wanting to try and eventually to succeed, he needs recognition, not only for what he has actually achieved but also for his effort; perhaps even more for his effort since achievement brings its own reward. Otherwise he may give up the struggle, preferring to remain babyish and dependent; or he may seek recognition in socially unacceptable ways.

Because learning, even for the intelligent child, is a slow and often arduous business, beset by difficulties and setbacks, a strong incentive is needed. This is provided by the pleasure shown at success and by the praise given to achievement by the adults whom the child loves and wants to please. Encouragement and a reasonable level of expectation act as a spur to effort and perseverance. Too low a level of expectation tends to make a child accept too low a standard of achievement; too high expectations lead to discouragement and diminished effort because he feels he cannot live up to what is required of him. To be optimal the level of expectation needs to be geared to each individual's capability at a given stage of growth, a level where success is possible but not without effort.

The need for responsibility and independence

The urge to become increasingly self-reliant and independent is a feature of normal development. This need is met by allowing the child to become responsible for himself in such simple matters as feeding, dressing and washing himself; later by granting him increasing freedom of movement without supervision, be it in the house, the street or neighbourhood; as well as by making him responsible for his own possessions, from toys and pets to money and clothes; and finally by letting him become entirely self-supporting until eventually he assumes responsibility for others. The child can only learn how to exercise responsibility and assume independence if he is deliberately given increasing opportunities to do so.

Learning and emotion

The goals of child rearing and education are basically similar, even though home and school emphasise different aspects. Broadly speaking, their aim is to ensure that children acquire maximal emotional stability so that they are resilient under the inevitable stresses and strains of life; and to promote the development of all their intellectual and educational potentialities so that they become fulfilled as individuals and effective as citizens. To achieve these aims the quality of the personal relationships available to a child during the most formative period of his life, the pre-school years, is of paramount importance. Growing up in a united, stable family where each child is cherished for his own sake; where standards for behaviour and achievements are provided which are appropriate to his age and ability; and where he experiences mutually satisfying and close relationships with his mother to begin with, then with his father and other members of the family: all these experiences form the basis for his later ability to make reciprocal, dependable and enjoyable relationships with an ever-widening circle of relatives and friends, both adults and children.

Just as he became willing to learn because he wanted to please his mother and retain her approval and affection, so he adjusts to school and applies himself to scholastic tasks to please his teacher. But this motivation tends to be lacking in children whose basic psychological needs have been inadequately met. For example, if they are preoccupied with stress-ful relationships to their parents or between their parents, learning to read or to do arithmetic is a problem of minor importance. Similarly, the tension created by feelings of jealousy, anxiety or hostility prevent children from organising their emotional energies for school learning. Thus anything which interferes with the satisfaction of the basic needs is likely to impair the capacity for educational achievement, be it in able or slow pupils; while the loved, secure child enjoys learning and is able to face stress, whatever his intellectual ability.

11. Maladjustment and Underachievement

'Happy childhood'

Most of us, as we grow older, forget how we saw the world and how we felt about people, especially those closest to us. The more we can remember, the easier it is to understand the behaviour of children. Being able to remember may well be the main quality possessed by those said to be 'good with children'. Many people prefer to paint a rosy picture of unclouded days of happiness, such wishful thinking acting perhaps as an antidote to the drabness and stresses of adult life. In reality, growing up is a difficult, and at times rather unhappy, business because of the child's very lack of experience: the younger he is, the more exclusively does he live in the present and the less can he draw comfort from a sense of perspective as well as from the knowledge which time will bring, that everything is transitory.

However much parents try to protect their child from frightening situations, however reasonable and loving they may be, however understanding and progressive a school they choose for him to attend, being alive and growing up bring their own problems. Learning to manage feelings, learning to make sense of a bewilderingly complex world and learning to find one's identity and place in it, bring both joy and misery. So it is inevitable that all children find it difficult from time to time to adjust to the demands and expectations of the adult world. What then is the difference between children with problems and problem children?

The concept of maladjustment

Labels are rather misleading since they suggest watertight compartments such as 'the normal' and the 'abnormal'. Hard-and-fast distinctions of this kind are quite artificial since the difference is one of degree and not of kind: the behaviour of the maladjusted child closely resembles the normal child's reaction to insecurity, jealousy, rejection, inconsistent handling, or whatever it may be; but he shows these reactions in an intensified form.

All children pass through phases of temporary maladjustment. Transient problem behaviour is so common as to be normal and it has in fact been argued that a child who has never shown any difficulties whatsoever, should be considered abnormal. The negativistic three-year-old who has made 'no' and 'shan't' his most frequently used phrases; the seven-year-old who is anxious about going into the big junior school; the thirteen-year-old who is moody and inconsistent—these reactions are characteristic of a particular age and stage of development.

Criteria

The first question to ask when judging problem behaviour is how common is it at a given age. Frequent temper tantrums are quite common in a four-year-old, are unusual in a seven-year-old, but are so rare in an eleven-year-old that at that age they are likely to indicate serious maladjustment. Chronological age is, then, the first criterion. This means viewing a child's behaviour in the light of developmental norms which have been obtained from the systematic study of large numbers of children at similar ages.

Age alone, however, is insufficient for judging the significance of behaviour which deviates from what is normal for a particular age group. A very able child will often show behaviour appropriate to one much older. For example, the eight-year-old who prefers his own company or that of adults to his contemporaries; who refuses to learn by rote; who will not admit defeat and cries angrily when unable to solve a problem he has set himself; who refuses to go to sleep because he never has enough time to complete what he wants to do; who is restless, inquisitive and bitterly resents interruptions; such a child is clearly out of step with those of his own age. When it becomes recognised that his all-round intelligence or, as some people prefer to call it, his educable capacity is similar to that of the average twelve-year-old, then his behaviour is seen to be part of a general developmental acceleration rather than symptomatic of emotional disturbance. Of course, high intellectual ability and maladjustment are by no means mutually exclusive.

Two further criteria are the intensity and the persistence of a particular symptom. A good many children have fears, tell lies and steal. After all, who can honestly say they have never 'pinched' a pencil or told a 'fib'? Indeed, the slang words make these offences sound less serious straight away! But emotional difficulties must be suspected when a child is so full of fears that no sooner does one disappear than another takes its place; or when he seems quite unable to tell the truth, even when it would be to his advantage; or when he persists in fabricating fantastic stories long after normal children have learned to distinguish between fact and fiction. Another example showing the significance of the intensity of a symptom is nailbiting. Research has shown that the great majority of children bite their nails at some time or other. However, few indeed do it to the extent of drawing blood. Such a degree of intensity is indicative of some serious disturbance rather than just a bad habit.

A fifth criterion is a child's home background. Adjustment does not take place in a vacuum and can be evaluated only in relation to a specific cultural and social setting. For example, take Tessa who lived in a high-delinquency area of condemned slum property. Her family's criminal record was unusually consistent even in such a district—both parents, three brothers and one sister had been in prison, borstal and approved schools respectively. By coming into conflict with the law, Tessa followed the family pattern. Her delinquencies were not symptoms of maladjustment but rather reflected a lack of moral and social training. This in no way implies that such antisocial behaviour should be condoned, but the measures needed for re-education and rehabilitation will be different from those appropriate for the maladjusted child. On the other hand, when twelve-year-old John, the son of a headmaster, was found to be spending his leisure time breaking open gas meters, this activity was likely to be the outward expression of strong inner conflicts; there could be little doubt that it was completely out of keeping with his family's standards and with the social and moral training which he had received.

Heredity versus environment

So much, then, for criteria or pointers which suggest that a child may be maladjusted. What about the causes of maladjustment? This question has for long been a field for fierce argument, with 'nature' and 'nurture' as the respective battle cries. Unfavourable environmental circumstances are blamed by one side, poor heredity is held responsible by the other school of thought. What evidence there is suggests that the truth is likely to be less simple.

On the one hand, nature allows such wide individual variations in intelligence and physical stamina, that the same is probably true of emotional stability. Individual differences in such traits as fear and affection are quite evident in the first year or two of life. Even the Dionne Quins, who were biologically similar and brought up almost identically, showed individual differences in social development by the time they were two years old.

On the other hand, there is ample evidence—from clinical, socio-

logical and psychological work—that a great deal of emotional maladjustment is related to, if not caused by, an unfavourable environment.
Lack of sufficient insight and support on the part of the parent or teacher
may be a decisive factor in whether or not the child is able to cope with a
stressful situation. There is also a measure of truth in the view that there
are no problem children, only problem parents or, sometimes, problem
teachers. Proof of this lies in the fact that after help has been given
emotional difficulties often clear up completely.

In practice, it is very difficult to arrive at clearcut conclusions about
the relative influence of heredity and environment—often either
explanation seems to serve equally well. For example, Michael may have
inherited his father's quick temper and irritability, but the boy's excessive aggressiveness may equally well be due to being continually subjected to outbursts of temper, coupled with the fact that boys tend to
identify themselves with their fathers.

Since, from the moment of birth, there is constant interaction between
hereditary and environmental influences, it is quite impossible in any
given case to attribute a child's difficulty solely to one or the other, or to
apportion the extent to which either factor is responsible. But it is
defeatist to emphasise the influence of heredity. A more hopeful and
constructive attitude comes from a belief in the positive influence which
environment can have at any stage of a child's development. This means
acting on the assumption that, in most cases, problem behaviour is due
to some adverse factors in the family or the environment and that given
help, readjustment can and will take place.

Conflict and learning

'Children must be allowed to do as they please, as conflict causes
problem behaviour.' This fallacy is quite unfairly attributed to the
teaching of modern psychology. Nothing could in fact be further from
the truth. Conflict is quite essential to growth. It only becomes harmful
when it poses a problem which is insoluble or which is inappropriate to
the child's age and ability. One could go further and argue that for any
development to take place, the child must learn to give up more primi-
tive behaviour for new, more mature satisfactions. The two-year-old
has to give up the comfort of being carried or wheeled about, for the
pleasure of independent locomotion; the five-year-old must inhibit the
inclination to grab what he wants, for the advantage of playing co-
operatively with others; the thirteen-year-old must resolve the conflict
between joining his friends and doing his homework, which will earn
him the approval of parents and teachers, better marks or whatever
satisfaction is most effective at the time. Of course, conflicts will not

invariably be solved in the more mature direction but then progress in any field rarely proceeds in a straight line.

The harm comes from inappropriate or insoluble conflict, the more so if it is chronic. A two-year-old cannot be expected to give up grabbing for the sake of sharing with others nor can the five-year-old be expected to choose doing homework instead of play; and there is no solution open to the child who is unwanted or whose loyalties are being competed for by quarrelling parents who openly disagree about his upbringing. Such conflicts undermine a child's sense of security and impede healthy growth because no constructive alternatives are available from which a choice can be made.

Frequently one is faced with the apparent paradox of one child who has survived an extremely unfavourable environment apparently unscathed while another has succumbed to far less adverse circumstances. The answer lies probably in the fact that the most stable and resilient are capable of overcoming even intense and prolonged stress. At the same time, everyone has a breaking point. And it is the child's more malleable personality which is more vulnerable and hence more likely to become irreparably warped than that of the mature adult. In addition to inborn differences in temperamental stability and intellectual potential, every child's development is from the beginning helped or hindered in varying degrees by the opportunities, afforded to him by his home and his school, to face appropriate choices and to resolve soluble conflicts.

The meaning and significance of symptoms

Just like pain, symptoms of maladjustment are a danger signal, a call for help; they indicate that there is intolerable tension between the personality and the environment. Withdrawal is as urgent a danger signal as aggression although the latter is more likely to be heeded because it constitutes a threat to adult authority. The range of possible symptoms is extremely wide: one child may be solitary, another may stammer, a third may be unmanageable, a fourth delight in ill-treating animals, a fifth may be full of fears, a sixth may steal, and so on. Yet basically symptoms fall into two broad categories: aggression or withdrawal, hitting or hiding, fight or flight. Some children habitually choose one mode of reaction, others oscillate between retreat and attack. But why does one child become aggressive and defiant when he cannot have his own way while another accepts frustration unprotestingly? What determines the choice of a particular reaction in a particular child or on a particular occasion?

To some extent habitual behaviour is determined initially by personality type. The physically and emotionally robust, confident and outgoing child is likely to adopt outgoing, aggressive methods whilst the gentle, unsure and retiring one is likely to choose retreat. At the outset, the majority are probably neither extremely confident nor excessively timid and try out various means of meeting a difficult situation. Experience will teach them which is the most effective or least painful way. For example, Helen finds that temper tantrums are a sure way of getting what she wants; John learns that being quiet and conciliatory is most successful and gains him approval; strong-willed Stephen is punished so severely for nonconformity that, in addition to realising it does not pay, he grows afraid of punishment as well as of his own aggression to such a degree that he retreats into babyish and dependent behaviour.

Thus the relative success of aggressive or withdrawn behaviour determines to a great extent which facet of the child's personality will find predominating expression. If he gains his ends more readily by one mode, he will persevere with this behaviour pattern. Hence the way in which the earliest attempts at nonconformity and independence are handled, has a vital influence on shaping later reactions to adult authority. By the time a child begins school the decisive choice between aggression and withdrawal has usually been made; the same choice is likely to be made in the school situation. This is one of the reasons why one meets with a purely educational or purely emotional problem more often in theory than in the classroom. The close link between learning and emotion is another.

Interpreting symptoms

Symptoms of maladjustment are perhaps most appropriately likened to a fever: a sign of malaise, of disease, indicating the need for careful examination and diagnosis but by itself providing little clue to what is wrong or to effective treatment. Knowing the symptoms does not provide the key to the underlying causes; nor does knowing the underlying causes make it possible to predict likely symptoms. Take for example, stealing: parental rejection may be the underlying cause with Ann; her parents wanted a boy and instead had a girl, and a rather timid and plain one at that. Peter, on the other hand, is subjected to harsh discipline by his ex-sergeant-major father and gives overt expression to his repressed feelings of aggression and defiance by stealing; and in Edward's case stealing is not so much a symptom of maladjustment as due to a feckless home where he has lacked moral training. Thus the same symptoms may have a variety of causes. Hence action appropriate in one case would be inapplicable, ineffective and possibly even harmful in another.

Conversely, the same underlying causes may find expression in different symptoms. For example, Alan, jealous of his brilliant, popular brother reacts by overconformity, timidity, bedwetting and underfunctioning at school; while Jennifer, faced with the same problem of jealousy, is spiteful and disobedient at home, but at school is overambitious and extremely hardworking. Thus the actual symptoms shown are almost diametrically opposed.

There are two further complications. Only when seen within the context of the child's whole life can the significance of a symptom be assessed. Shyness, for example, may be the outward expression of anxieties and fears which have crippled a child's ability to make relationships with others; or it may only be the behaviour of a child who has plenty of interests and inner resources, which make him somewhat self-sufficient so that he does not need to take the first step in social relations though he has no real difficulty in making them. While a third child's shyness contains the seeds of real withdrawal though he is still seeking and gaining some satisfaction from contact with others.

Multiplicity of causation

Perhaps most fundamental of all is the fact that problem behaviour is rarely, if ever, due to one single cause or circumstance. Rather there is always a multiplicity of interrelated and interacting factors which eventually lead to maladjustment. For this reason there is no short cut either to diagnosis or to treatment. The health, appearance, intelligence and whole personality of the child; the economic, social and cultural standing of his parents; the relationship between them and between all the other members of the family; the child's experiences at school and in the neighbourhood—all these and many more factors play a part. Their combination and impact are unique for each child. Thus the relative importance of a particular set of circumstances differs for each child even in the same family as does the aspect most likely to respond to intervention or therapy.

In practice nuisance value or social unacceptability still tend to be used as the main criteria of problem behaviour. This leads to two undesirable consequences: the aggressive child who hits back tends to arouse aggression in the adults concerned; this leads to a vicious circle of increasingly severe punishment calling out increasing aggression in the child who grows hardened to punishment, which then loses its effectiveness. Secondly, the withdrawn, overconforming child tends to be overlooked though he will receive more sympathetic handling. His real needs are even more likely to remain unmet since the understanding that a child can be 'too good' has been slow in coming.

No generally acceptable definition exists of a mentally healthy child but there would probably be general agreement that a confident, enquiring attitude of mind and the ability to make mutually rewarding relationships both with adults and peers are essential characteristics. Viewed in this context, the anxious, timid, always obedient child must cause concern. In fact, fight or flight, aggression or withdrawal, need to be regarded as equally significant danger signs, indicating that a child's emotional, social or intellectual needs are not being met adequately.

The concept of underachievement

While backwardness relates educational attainments to chronological age and hence to the level of work reached by the majority of a child's contemporaries, underachievement or underfunctioning relates it solely to the capacity of the individual pupil. In the one case a group norm serves as the yardstick, in the other it is the learning ability of the particular child in question.

The needs of children who are either educationally backward, slow learning or both, have received considerable attention in recent years. Though provision to meet their needs still remains inadequate, at least they are fairly well understood. This is by no means the case with regard to underachievement. Far too often it is still thought—by parents and even by teachers—that if a child does badly at school he must be either stupid or lazy or possibly both; large classes and inexperienced teachers are also made to take a share of the blame. That intellectually able or very able children may in their schoolwork not reach the level of their own potential or fail to achieve even the level of the majority of their own age group, is an idea which has been particularly slow in gaining acceptance.

It is generally realised that exceptionally intelligent children can hardly be expected to function at a level commensurate with their mental age. For one thing, it is unlikely that they will be taught at so advanced a stage; for another, it is by no means established that the teaching appropriate for the average fifteen-year-old is equally suitable—qualitatively or quantitatively—to the ten-year-old who has a mental age of fifteen years. Moreover, for the most outstandingly gifted, such as a mathematical genius, the commonly used standards of attainment are not applicable anyhow.

Be that as it may, the education of able children generally and the needs of able underfunctioning children in particular have so far received only limited consideration in Britain. Though grammar schools are designed to cater for the top 25 to 30 per cent of an age group, rarely if ever do they make special provision for those who fall behind or fail to cope with the traditional curriculum. The able child who is seriously underfunctioning in the primary school will not gain entry to a grammar school at all, however high his intelligence.

Placed and taught together with pupils of much more limited ability than himself, boredom with too slow a pace and too pedestrian a teaching approach is likely to worsen his plight. As often as not his intellectual capacity will be underestimated, since teachers tend to judge it largely by educational achievement. Even if group intelligence tests are used, one of two things may happen: because such tests resemble ordinary school tasks, the child who has an unfavourable attitude to the latter, who lacks concentration and quickly loses interest, will probably not do himself justice; if, on the other hand, the test captures his imagination and he does well, the chances are that his teacher will suspect he may have cheated or else doubt the validity of this particular test result.

If an able pupil shines in oral work, or if his teacher is exceptionally perceptive in spotting the occasional outstanding thought or idea, then the underfunctioning child will be detected in school. Sometimes his parents may grow concerned when they had thought him promising and then find his school work to be only mediocre. In other cases it is behaviour difficulties which gain him special attention and which then bring to light that he is also an underachiever.

Causes of underachievement
Rarely can educational difficulties be ascribed to one cause alone. Not only is there almost invariably a multiplicity of interacting and interdependent factors, but because of the close link between emotion and learning, scholastic failure is usually accompanied by behaviour difficulties of one kind or another. Since the basis of all learning is laid in the home during the earliest years of life, the chances are high that the roots of underachievement are also to be found there. Parental attitudes to the child, to achievement in general and to scholastic success in particular, as well as their own level of education and the cultural stimulation they provided during the pre-school years and thereafter, play a major part. The child's own personality and how it interacts with and is influenced by that of his brothers and sisters further affects progress. Emotional relationships within the family, between the parents, and between them and the child also have a vital role. And none of these operate in isolation but in their unique combination they affect emotional and intellectual development, and hence the child's readiness, adaptation and responsiveness to the school situation.

This in turn may be favourable or inimical to his particular needs. If he is fortunate it will build on and supplement what his home has given him so far, thus extending his range of emotional relationships as well as his intellectual horizons. At worst, it may extinguish his curiosity and his delight in learning, because of an uninspired teaching approach, because there is failure in personal relations, or because of a combination of these. Extremes being rare, the most likely situation will be somewhere in between.

Treatment of underachievement

Given the complexity of causation, simple coaching in a particular school subject is unlikely to meet with much success. The teacher who sees his role in a wider framework than the inculcating of skills and the purveying of information, is in a position of great influence. He can counteract or at least mitigate the unfavourable consequences of an emotionally or culturally unfavourable home background; he can kindle the latent enthusiasm of the able child for intellectual pursuits, harness his emotional energies by giving praise and recognition, and compensate him for emotional deprivation by offering affection, albeit of a less 'exclusive' and close nature than parental love. Of course, the larger the class and the more deprived the child, the more difficult it is for the teacher to give the required time and attention to an individual pupil. In any case, specialist help may be needed if only in order to involve the parents and influence their attitudes.

The effect of emotion on learning needs to be given much greater practical recognition, both by parents and teachers. In the classroom, material to be learned needs to be related to the self-concept and level of aspiration of the learner. Research has shown that the successful pupil tends to set his aspirations at a realistic level, whereas the failing child is liable to set them too high or too low. Moreover, if he is made to feel unduly guilty or anxious because of his failure, he often becomes more concerned about finding ways to avoid feeling this anxiety than about understanding the reasons for his failure. Whatever their level of ability, children need to experience in their learning the stimulus of success as well as the discipline of failure, without being overwhelmed by guilt or anxiety. Divorcing or isolating the intellectual from the emotional side of life, is unlikely to lead to successful learning. Only a minority of pupils can be taught to the limits of their ability when their feelings remain uninvolved.

12. Able Misfits—The Findings of Previous Research

Exactly how many children fail to make the most of their abilities and the causes for their failure, remain unanswered questions, largely because interest in such children has been sporadic, particularly in this country. One study (Parkyn, 1948) indicated that 'a rather large proportion—about a quarter—of the highly intelligent group failed to do as well as was desired'. It has also been suggested that high intelligence may itself be a handicap in adjusting to school life. 'Children up to about an I.Q. of 140 tolerate the ordinary school routine fairly well ... but above this status, children become increasingly bored with school work, if kept in or nearly in the lockstep' (Hollingworth, 1942). Nor is there any consensus of opinion on whether able children should be educated at special schools or whether the advantage lies with giving them special attention and tuition in ordinary schools.

Sex differences

Just as in the general population a higher proportion of boys than girls are reported to have educational and emotional difficulties, so it is among able children (Nevill, 1937; Conklin, 1940; McLaren, 1949; Burns, 1949; Nason, 1958; and Chazan, 1959). There is as yet no generally accepted explanation for this fact, either with regard to children in general or the bright in particular. Current hypotheses cover the whole spectrum; from viewing boys as being more vulnerable right from birth onwards (Butler and Bonham, 1964; Butler and Alberman, 1968; Pringle, Butler and Davie, 1966) to ascribing the difference between the sexes to differential cultural expectations and environmental conditioning.

Position in the family

Many studies have shown that among gifted children the proportion of first-borns is much higher than in the population at large (Terman, 1925; Musselman, 1942; McLaren, 1949; Roe, 1953; Barbe, 1956b;

Drews and Teahan, 1957; Shertzer, 1960; Pierce and Bowman, 1960). One study (Cicirelli, 1967) suggests that birth order is unrelated to ability and achievement in families where there are three or more siblings, but plays a part in two-child families; also, that while later born children do better in the early school years, first-borns come to the fore during their secondary stage and at college.

Though the preponderance of first-borns seems to be quite a well-documented and non-controversial finding, there is little consensus on why they are more creative, productive or eminent, particularly as adults. Some writers question whether birth order has any psychological significance at all. In a review of the literature on this topic, Schachter (1963) goes as far as claiming that 'the repeated findings of a surplus of first-borns among eminent scholars appears to have nothing to do with any direct relationship of birth order to eminence, but is simply a reflection of the fact that scholars, eminent or not, derive from a population in which first-borns are in marked surplus'.

It is rather unlikely, that birth order has no influence on personality development, whatever a child's intellectual endowment may be. A number of possible explanations have been put forward, and they are not mutually exclusive. One interpretation may be that first-borns are conceived and reared at a time when parental vigour, both physical and intellectual, is likely to be optimal; another, that the parents, but particularly the mother, have more time and energy to devote to the first-born who is likely to remain an only child for about a year, if not longer, and thus enjoys undivided attention; yet another interpretation stresses that first-born children are likely to be overprotected because their parents are relatively inexperienced; overanxiety about their development and progress may also be more common for the same reason; it is possible too, that first-borns tend to be more competitive because they internalise their parents' high hopes for them or because jealousy of subsequent arrivals expresses itself in a desire to excel and beat any competitors (including younger brothers and sisters). All or any of these factors may promote the fullest realisation of a child's potential, not least because he is given a headstart during the early, most formative years of his life.

Educational difficulties

Generally speaking, able children do better in reading than in arithmetic, particularly mechanical arithmetic (Terman, 1925; Conklin, 1940; Lewis, 1943; Cutts and Moseley, 1957; Parkyn, 1948; McLaren, 1949; Gallagher and Crowder, 1957). The explanation most commonly advanced is that bright pupils are used to learning quickly and dislike work which must be done slowly and accurately. Added to this is their distaste for repetitive work which is so often a feature of arithmetic teaching. Moreover, even the brightest children cannot advance further than the majority, if they have not yet had the opportunity of learning more advanced processes.

With regard to poor readers it is thought (Barbe, 1956a) that bright children tend to become bored if given too easy books to read. Their ready ability to memorise enables them to get by for quite a time since they may be able to repeat a story almost verbatim after hearing it just once.

There is some evidence that boredom characterises the able pupil's general attitude to school. 'Not infrequently the superior child is unable to adapt himself to the dull routine of drill that is characteristic of many classrooms. He may lose interest or deliberately rebel against what he considers useless activity' (Sumption and Luecking, 1960). This tends to show itself in one of three ways: withdrawal from class activity and refusal to participate in the work, particularly when he is required to repeat what he already knows; nonconformity by deliberately challenging the teacher's authority or by adopting a negative attitude on all issues; and, the most common of the three attitudes, doing just enough to ensure that he will not be bothered by the teacher; as a result he is often rated average or below but without being considered a real failure.

Behaviour difficulties

These have been explored mainly in relation to children referred to child guidance clinics (Burns, 1949; McLaren, 1949; Chazan, 1959). Hence the incidence of maladjustment found was inevitably high. The presenting symptoms covered the whole spectrum of nervous, habit and behaviour disorders, but the proportion of children showing particular syndromes differed quite widely from one study to another (Table V, p. 112).

The relation between educational and behaviour difficulties

There is general agreement that although emotional and learning difficulties are frequently found together, it is impossible to determine which is cause and which effect because of their close interrelation. Two studies (Haggard, 1957; D'Heurle et al., 1959) explored the hypothesis that children who show a similar pattern of academic achievement also share similarities in personality development. Arithmetic, they argued, involves the understanding of abstract, symbolic relationships and hence requires controlled intellectual manipulation. Reading involves the comprehension of verbal stimuli and symbolic meanings and hence is fostered by intellectual imagination and fantasy; spelling is mastered largely by memorisation, by following rules, and by attention to detail, hence it requires intellectual passivity.

Their findings lend support to these hypotheses. Children who showed high achievement in arithmetic but low achievement in reading were more skilled in objective reasoning, more responsive in personal relationships and more self-assertive, compared with those who showed the opposite pattern of achievement, i.e. high reading and low arithmetic.

Children who did well in arithmetic but were poor spellers showed greater spontaneity and independence, and were more active and academic than those whose achievement pattern was reversed, low arithmetic and high spelling. Lastly, good readers with poor spelling showed more independence, a richer fantasy life and more skill in handling verbal and symbolic stimuli than good spellers with poor reading attainment.

In another study a comparison was made between 'The bright achiever and under-achiever' (Pierce, 1962). Its aim was to explore the hypothesis that variability in achievement among equally able children could be accounted for in terms of differing degrees of adjustment and willingness to comply with the demands of the school situation. The pupils were nearing the end of their high school careers. Underachievers were found to be less adjusted socially and emotionally; were more aggressive and had a greater dislike of school; had less developed qualities of leadership; and lower educational and occupational ambitions than those whose school achievements were satisfactory.

Learning difficulties, home background and family relationships

The fact that 'gifted children are rarely found in the lowest occupational levels' has long been recognised (Terman et al., 1930). Later studies, confirming this finding, emphasise that the difference may lie not so much in the actual incidence, but in the detection of high ability which in turn is likely to be due to potential gifts remaining unrealised because of an unstimulating home environment. Thus, 'the high correlation between the gifted child's economic and cultural environment and the emergence of his giftedness is an indication of the influence of early environmental factors' (Witty, 1951). There is a similar trend with regard to able children who have learning difficulties (Lewis, 1941; McLaren, 1949; Chazan, 1959).

That very high ability may win through despite severely adverse conditions in childhood, is demonstrated by the early lives of many

Table V. Behaviour Difficulties of Intelligent Children

Author	McLaren (1949) N = 200 retarded 8½ to 13½ Mean 11–2 (per cent)	McLaren (1949) N = 100 not re-tarded 8½ to 13½ Mean 11–2 (per cent)	Burns (1949) N = 87 10–2 to 16–8 Mean 13–2 (per cent)	Chazan (1959) N = 60 Mean 14–0 (per cent)	Pringle (1970) N = 103 5 to 17 Mean 10–7 (per cent)
Nervous					
Solitary	15·5	12			25
Withdrawn, inhibited	24·5	12		10	23
Unresponsive	19·5	6			22
Restless	29·5	24			6
Overtimid	12·0	11	9		28
Highly strung	12·5	10	17		25
Phobias			1		9
Anxious	31·5	35	10	3	45
Psychopathic or psychotic			9		

Habit					
5					
Speech	14			3	9
Disturbed sleep/walk	23·5	19			6
Nervous mannerisms	17·5	15			18
Nail biting	9·5	22			6
Food fads		9			2
Wetting and soiling	21·5	21			3
Asthma				5	6
Behaviour					
Attention-seeking, exhibitionistic	16·0	7			11
Unmanageable, disobedient	19·5	17		27	16
Temper tantrums	12·0	11			17
Aggressive destruction	28·0	11	16		24
Stealing	25·0	20	17	15	8
Truancy	17·5	16	10	17	6
Day dreaming	24·0	17			21
Lack of concentration	30·5	11			29
Jealousy	7·0	20			17

geniuses, such as Faraday or Dickens; but those somewhat less able may well be overwhelmed by environmental odds, the more so, the earlier their onset. Hence general ability and talent well above the average may never declare themselves if adequate nurture is lacking or if emotional deprivation is severe.

In recent years the emphasis has rather shifted from the influence of socio-economic factors as such to those relating to the quality of parental interest and encouragement (Floud, Halsey and Martin, 1957; Douglas, 1964; Douglas *et al.*, 1968; Gooch and Pringle, 1966). Of course, the relationship between socio-economic level and parental interest in the child's progress is recognised, as is the fact that family relationships and the emotional climate of the home may be of overriding importance, be they negative or positive in their effect.

The achievement motive—what makes children want to do well—has received increasing attention since the mid-fifties (McClelland *et al.*, 1953; McClelland, 1955). It has been argued that for children to develop high achievement motivation, parents must provide opportunities for mastery at a level of expectation just beyond the child's present knowledge or attainment. Such high parental expectations together with a deliberate training for independence, both physical and intellectual, are thought to promote actual achievement (Barrett, 1957; Gowan, 1957).

It is generally agreed that through the process of identification children tend to adopt the value system of the parent who is of the same sex as themselves: hence boys generally introject the standards and ideals of their fathers, and girls those of their mothers. The same was found to be true of 'achieving and non-achieving gifted children' (Pierce and Bowman, 1960; Norman, 1966).

In another study, 'Differences in home background between high-achieving and low-achieving children' (McGillivray, 1964), parental knowledge and ambition in relation to education, together with a willingness to pay university fees were shown to be of much more importance than size of family, housing and income; with regard to personality factors, among high-achievers a greater proportion of mothers were the dominant partner whereas among low-achievers it was more often the father. 'The hypothesis that supportive family relations foster academic achievement via promoting positive attitudes towards teachers, school and intellectual activities as symbols of the adult world of parents' is concluded by Morrow and Wilson (1961), as it was many years earlier by Wilson (1949) and Conklin (1940).

Disruption in family structure and relationships has been found to be associated with underachievement among able children by a number of workers (Terman and Oden, 1947; Roe, 1953; and Frankel, 1960). Among able children referred to child guidance clinics for behaviour difficulties the picture was very similar. Unfavourable parental attitudes, inconsistent handling and lack of interest in the child's progress were commonly reported (Thom and Newell, 1945; Chazan, 1959).

Reviewing the causes of failure among gifted children, Burt (1962b) concluded that 'by far the most important factors arose from those emotional elements of personality which underlie motivation and in particular from the child's attitude towards school . . . In many cases the school itself is largely to blame: the deep and lasting influence, exercised by an enthusiastic and scholarly teacher, is constantly mentioned in the autobiographical or retrospective comments of pupils who have effectively developed their potential gifts; the lack of a sympathetic teacher by those who have felt frustrated. Still more frequently . . . the favourable or unfavourable attitude of the child is determined by the attitude prevailing in the home. . . . Many of the parents appeared entirely indifferent to the child's success either in school or even in later life.'

Identifying able misfits

Whatever tests of general and special abilities may be used, and however varied their content to allow scope for the verbal and the technical mind, the analytic as well as the intuitive, the creative and not only the assimilative, the converger and the diverger—the focus must be on the child as a whole. This means that there is no short cut and no standardised substitute for the continued observations of an experienced teacher during his daily contacts with each pupil both in the classroom and outside it.

For parents this is a rather more difficult task for two reasons: they are, rightly and inevitably, much more emotionally involved with their own children and thus less able to make a detached appraisal; secondly, they lack the teachers' broad knowledge of child development and their wide experience of the range of abilities commonly found among children at various stages of growth. At the same time just because parents build up a deep and continuous relationship with the child from the earliest years, they not only play a vital part in fostering intellectual abilities but can help in identifying unrealised potentialities.

There is evidence to suggest that even in the most developed and affluent countries, including the United Kingdom, a proportion of able children remain unidentified throughout their school career. There are a number of reasons why this is so: the inadequacy of existing tests and other measuring devices; the cost of providing the necessary facilities

5*

since, in addition to screening procedures suitable for groups of children, individual diagnostic procedures by highly skilled staff are essential; and the move towards the establishment of a meritocracy which tends to be opposed to making exceptional educational provision for exceptional individuals (Pegnato, 1959; Martinson, 1966).

The identification of able but underachieving or emotionally disturbed children is even less well developed or systematic. Though the onset of academic underachieving can be detected quite early in a pupil's school life (Barrett, 1957; D'Heurle *et al.*, 1959; Shaw and McCuen, 1960; Nash, 1964), steps to diagnose and treat it are more likely to be taken during the secondary stage of education. Yet there is universal agreement, that the later an able underachiever is identified, the more difficult and lengthy the process of rehabilitation is likely to be—even if it proves successful eventually.

Teaching or treatment

There has been a tendency for educational adminstrators as well as teachers themselves to concentrate special attention (and special provision) on children of limited mental ability. The (often unstated) assumption is that those of superior or high ability are capable of developing and functioning adequately without requiring any special attention. Yet it has been argued (Havighurst *et al.*, 1955) that 'at least half of our best human material is not developed to anywhere near capacity'. Whether the proportion is as high in this country as in the USA (to which the author just quoted refers) is not known. Be this as it may, much more has been written on the causes of underachievement than on possible cures, let alone their tested effectiveness.

The bright underachiever is frequently described as 'not trying hard enough' and it is asserted that he 'could if he would'. All too often it is an oversimplification to expect that exhortation or punishment will help to overcome the problem; even new administrative provision such as streaming or unstreaming, or a different set of teaching materials or methods may not bring about more than a temporary improvement.

When it comes to more specialised or intensive measures, the situation is not much more clear-cut either. There is conflicting evidence on whether teaching or treatment is more appropriate; and also, more specifically, whether it should be teaching in a mixed ability group, in a class of able children or actual remedial teaching; and whether non-directive counselling or intensive psychiatric methods of one kind or another is more likely to lead to improved educational functioning. There is more general agreement on the fact that emotional factors prevent able children from realising their potential more often than poor teaching, absence from school or conditions related to classroom organisation.

Some studies report encouraging improvement when specially skilled teachers or specially designed methods were used to bring about both higher educational achievement and a more favourable attitude to learning in general (Passow and Goldberg, 1963; Karnes *et al.*, 1963). Other reports are far less hopeful, the more so, the later help was made available (Peterson, 1966; Raph *et al.*, 1966).

A variety of approaches was used in one large scale study in New York, called the Talent Preservation Project (Krugman, 1960). These ranged from special teaching methods and compensatory, culturally enriching programmes to family casework and group therapy. Some improvement apparently took place almost immediately: many children, who had not considered themselves able, began to do better as soon as they were told the test results; many families, who previously had not intended to let their boys and girls go on to college, were prepared to reconsider their attitude; and teachers themselves changed their techniques when made aware of their pupil's potential. It is a pity that the design of the project did not make it possible to compare the effectiveness of these various approaches. An assessment will be made, however, of the extent to which the educational level of these gifted underachievers has been improved.

Whether or not counselling can directly affect learning performance is still largely an open question (Raph *et al.*, 1966). Findings from New Zealand suggest that non-directive counselling, given both individually and to small groups on school premises, does result in significant educational and emotional improvements (Shouksmith and Taylor, 1964). A group of able but underachieving pupils was matched with two control groups, neither of whom received counselling and there was no change in their achievement level. There was also an improvement in the social adjustment and attitude to school work in the group who had received this help over a six-month period.

Yet the results of other attempts to assess the effects of vocational counselling and group therapy on scholastic underachievers have proved disappointing (Harris and Trolta, 1962; Keppers and Caplan, 1962). Though there was some improvement, this was not marked enough to recommend these approaches with any degree of confidence.

PART 4

Practical Implications

A discussion of social policy is presented in this part, with particular emphasis on prevention and remedial action. The findings of research are related to the practical implications which these have for educational and social provision for the able child.

13. The Present Situation

Early detection

There is general agreement that it is important to start identifying potentially very able children at the earliest possible age. This means at the latest when they start school so that teaching methods and a curriculum suited to their unusual capacities can be provided for them. To wait until the secondary stage is leaving it too late, even though some very specific interests and gifts may be late in maturing. It is equally important that the able underachieving child is detected as early as possible: not only because educational failure is cumulative and thus more difficult to reverse, the later it is tackled; but also, because the emotional and social concomitants of failure require more skilled and prolonged attention, the longer they have been operative.

Can we afford it?

It might be argued that at a time of teacher shortage and economic stringency, any additional education and care must be devoted to the mentally and physically handicapped, once the needs of normal children are satisfactorily provided for. Yet in the interest of economic and even national survival, may it not be the highly intelligent few who will be making the greatest contribution? 'In our laudable anxiety to improve the lot of our own generation, we are apt to close our eyes to the effects of present policy on the generations to come. . . . The influence of great men on the course of history is a well-worn platitude. But too often both historian and biographer have allowed us to forget the many occasions on which disaster has befallen nations and empires just because the great man was not forthcoming at the crucial moment' (Burt, 1962b).

The extent of underachievement

How widespread then is the present loss or waste of high ability? Our present state of knowledge comes from two types of sources, direct and inferred evidence. The direct evidence derives from studies of under-achieving able children and is largely based on comparatively small-scale enquiries, many of which are case studies (see chapter 12). These have shown the various conditions most commonly associated with this type of underachievement: an unstimulating home background; lack of early training which encourages a desire for achievement; an over-ambitious home where learning becomes a source of anxiety instead of enjoyment; unhappy family relationships, whether between child and parents, or between the parents themselves; and schooling which fails to arouse and engage the child's interests. The characteristics most commonly found among the children themselves are: a sense of inade-quacy and limited ambitions; a dislike of school and book learning; poor work habits; unsatisfactory relationships with their contemporaries; and a high incidence of emotional difficulties.

It is clear, however, that this direct evidence represents only the tip of an iceberg. The indirect evidence gives a better approximation as to the likely extent of underachievement among potentially able children. This is provided by a number of different sources. One is the record of immigrant groups in a new country which offers them greater economic opportunity than they had had in their own. For example, 'the second and third generations in the United States born of European immigrants produce more children who score high in intelligence tests, and who complete a university course, than does the first generation. Presumably they do this by bettering their economic circumstances, and then bettering their homes as places for rearing talented children' (Havig-hurst, 1962).

Another source is the study of adopted or of foster-children who have been brought up in homes, superior in intellectual and cultural stimula-tion to those which their biological parents would have provided for them. Such children come to resemble more closely the intellectual level of their foster-parents. Similar results have been found in studies of identical twins who have been reared apart; the one brought up in a more favourable environment showing higher performance than his less fortunate identical twin. (Dinnage and Pringle, 1967, Pringle, 1967),

Yet another source of underdeveloped talent is among girls. About two-thirds of the pupils who leave school early, though they have the ability to proceed further, are girls. No evidence has been produced since this official figure was given to show that there has been any material improvement in the proportion of girls, compared with boys, going on to further or higher education (*Early Leaving*, Report by the Central Advisory Council for Education, HMSO, 1954). Many parents, especially in the lower income groups, believe there is little point in girls staying on at school beyond the statutory leaving age.

A rather different type of evidence, supporting the view that potential ability or talent can be fostered by providing a stimulating, nurturing environment comes from the fact that specific cultural groups tend to produce specific kinds of talent. 'For instance, talented musicians come frequently from Italian families, while talented physical scientists have come more frequently from North European countries. Whenever a cultural group places a high value on a certain form of art or on human performance in any other area, it is likely to produce more high-level performers in this area than other groups which do not value this particular form of performance so highly. This is true also in the area of athletic performance, as can be seen by examining the records of various countries in the Olympic Games' (Havighurst, 1962).

High ability—an underutilised reservoir

In general terms, then, there is sufficient evidence that even in advanced countries there is quite a reservoir of unutilised or underdeveloped high ability. But there is an urgent need to define with greater clarity the concepts and terms in current use, such as high ability, talent, giftedness and creativity; to determine whether there is any relationship between any or all of them; and to explore the best climate and methods for developing them, at home and in school, formally and informally. Also it is essential to adopt a multidisciplinary and interaction frame of reference.

'In the past, sociologists, psychologists and educators have sometimes taken up positions which have implied that either the individual differences alone, or the character of the environmental situation (both physical and social) alone, accounted for most of the variations in behaviour. But behaviour is determined by both the individual and the situation and by the interaction between them. . . . Obviously the research and methodological approaches needed to study the talented are complex. Often they will involve multivariate analysis and always they will be time-consuming. Some of the most noteworthy will be longitudinal studies. Many will be concerned with the process and not just with product or content. But such involved and lengthy studies are appropriate to the importance, the magnitude and the complexity of the problems' (Drews, 1962).

Current knowledge and understanding

The current state of knowledge was best summed up by Burt (1962a), and what he said then, remains as true today: 'The problem of the

gifted child turns out to be unexpectedly complex. Heredity and environment, intelligence and motivation are inextricably involved . . .
Facts, however, are still in short supply.' This applies even more to the
able child who has learning or behaviour difficulties, and thus fails to
realise his potential to the full. Discussing where the loss of talent occurs,
the same author (1962b) cites an investigation undertaken for the
National Science Foundation in the USA (Bridgman, 1960). Its results
indicated 'the measure of our failure as educators at the present day'.
Burt urges 'that it is high time a similar set of inquiries were undertaken
in Britain'.

Some American workers consider that enough is now known about
the conditions associated with lack of educational success among able
pupils. 'There are surprisingly few contradictions in the picture of the
underachiever as painted by the various studies. The characteristics
that distinguish the underachiever are not superficial ones; they involve
the deepest roots of personality. One could generalise that most of them
can be accounted for by either an intellectually sterile background in
the home and early grades, or an emotionally frustrating background
arising from inter-personal tensions at home and at school' (Gold, 1965).
Therefore, it is argued, the time has come to face and accept the situation,
and make plans for action.

'The fact of bona fide underachievement of many gifted children has
been re-established. The characteristics of the condition have been
reasonably well redemonstrated, although some dynamic factors in the
condition can still be better delineated. But enough is known to warrant
the next step, the experimental validation of appropriate remedial
education techniques' (Newland, 1963).

Remedial techniques and other teatment
This had in fact been done in 1950 when a collaborative, long-term study
entitled 'The Talented Youth Project', was launched in the United
States, and a first volume of findings has appeared (Raph, Goldberg
and Passow, 1966). Perhaps the main conclusion, which has emerged
from some twelve years' work, is that there are no easy answers. Inspired
teachers helped some children; remedial methods were successful with
others; special grouping improved the performance of yet other underachievers; and counselling also brought increased success to some. The
team's overall conclusion is that the subject of underachievement is in
need of considerably more study. If its nature is to be more clearly
understood and its consequences modified, then much more attention
must be paid to the learning which takes place in early childhood rather
than during adolescence.

Underachievers in the UK

What about the situation in Britain? Until selective secondary education began to give way to comprehensive education, some people argued that selection, based on objective methods and not the financial means of parents, had reduced the incidence of underachievement very significantly and this would increasingly continue to be the case. Others—pointing to the very different proportions of children winning competitive entry to grammar schools from middle-class homes as compared with those from a working-class background—argued for the existence of a large pool of untapped ability.

A middle position was taken by Wall (1960) in a survey of the needs of highly intelligent children. 'By and large, our process for the identification of high ability of the kind necessary to success in our educational system and in general in many—but not all—the walks of life probably works efficiently in one direction. . . . On the other hand, very little is known of the kinds of negative selection that go on, about the proportions and kinds of children who are eliminated at various stages either because their forms of thinking are not appropriate to the education they are given or because they fall behind at one stage of their growth and do not catch up again.'

So at present we just do not know the size of the problem of underachievement. There have been local, regional and even national surveys from time to time but none has addressed itself to this question. It is only quite recently that a first national study of very able children (undertaken by the National Bureau for Co-operation in Child Care, and described in its *Annual Report*, 1968–9) has been started in this country. Another study, undertaken by the University of Liverpool Department of Education and concerned with providing and evaluating a specially designed, enriched curriculum for highly intelligent pupils, is also now underway.

Lastly, what is the relevance of our own study of 103 able misfits to the problem of underachievement among intelligent children? On the one hand, it is a small and highly selected group. On the other hand, our findings corroborate those of other studies and perhaps throw some additional light on some types of family patterns found among able misfits. The four groups described in the case studies are not mutually exclusive since, for example, one parent may have too high and the other too low expectations. Also, a different classification could have been used, focusing, for example, on whether or not there was a tradition of excellence in the home. Then it could have been shown that some children came from such homes and indeed, good intelligence in their offspring was taken for granted by the parents (for example, Betty, case study No. 13, p. 52); that some had homes without such tradition but which welcomed and admired the child's excellence (for example Charles, case study No. 9, p. 38); that others not only lacked such tradition but were quite indifferent to it (for example, Albert, case Study No. 11, p. 44); while a number of children had parents who were hostile and indeed despised intellectual prowess (for example, Paul, case study No. 12, p. 49).

The next steps

There are three questions which need to be answered if effective help is to be provided for able children who have emotional and educational difficulties. First, the size of the problem must be established so that realistic plans can be made for overcoming it. Secondly, appropriate diagnostic tools need to be devised, and the different remedial and therapeutic approaches will have to be evaluated in the light of their success with such children. And thirdly, studies are needed of those able children who confound prediction: those who despite an unfavourable home background or uninspiring teaching do well during their school career, as well as those who subsequently excel themselves even though their scholastic performance had been consistently undistinguished. For too long the emphasis has been on failure or maladjustment —in this as in other fields, such as delinquency, maladjustment and backwardness—so that we have neglected the opportunity to learn from those children who do well despite similarly adverse experiences. Effective preventive measures are unlikely to be developed until it is discovered why many children who have been exposed to depriving or otherwise harmful environmental conditions nevertheless fully develop their potential. Again, an attempt to do this is now under way in a series of linked, developmental studies.[1]

To mount a regional or national enquiry into the incidence of underachievement among very able children would be a costly and rather difficult task; to do so when the children are young enough to allow for remedial and therapeutic measures to be applied with a reasonable chance of success, would be even more costly and difficult. But it could well be argued that the long-term benefits—and not merely those which can be assessed in financial terms—would considerably outweigh the costs of such a project.

[1] The National Child Development Study (1958 Cohort) and related studies of special groups, including adopted, physically handicapped and socially disadvantaged children. Details about all these projects are contained in the Annual Report 1968–9 of the National Bureau for Co-operation in Child Care.

14. Can the Number of Able Misfits be Reduced?

The starting point

Much remains to be learned about how best to promote the development of able children. But enough is known already to justify taking action now. It needs to be on two fronts simultaneously, preventive and rehabilitative, and in each case the earlier it is attempted the higher the chance of its success. Preventive action would aim at the early identification of able children to ensure an optimal environment for the development of their potentialities. Rehabilitation would aim at an early detection of able misfits so that appropriate help can be given before the difficulties have become too intractable.

The belief that many an able man or woman was only a mediocre scholar, showing little promise in any direction, is a comforting myth at best and at worst an indictment of either the home, the school or both. A comforting myth since, if believed, there is hope yet for our children, and possibly even ourselves, provided opportunity knocks. An indictment since, if ability is revealed later in life, it must have been present from the start. Hence parents and teachers failed to be alert to it, to evoke and then foster it. Retrospective accounts made by or about outstanding people are suspect since both memory and hindsight are selective. And this selectivity is in turn influenced by the argument being put forward. To give just two examples: if it is to show how mistaken, even blind, parents and teachers had been, then evidence will be adduced to prove how many signs of promise were in fact present at an early age; if it is to extol the virtues of the 'self-made' man or the uselessness of school learning, then evidence will be cited to prove that it is the 'school of life' and 'one's own unaided effort' which count for the most.

The fact is that all human growth and development are gradual, and by no means always even; neither the criminal nor the genius spring into life fully fledged. Some early signs of ability are almost always shown, unless a child grows up in a totally unstimulating or emotionally depriving environment. For such early signs to grow unnoticed, or to be

discouraged even, is much more common. What then are signs of ability?
And what is meant by early? There are of course many different abilities,
from artistic, athletic, moral and political, to general intellectual ability
and academic achievements of various kinds. It is primarily the latter
two with which we are concerned here and it is on these on which most
attention has focused in relation to underachievement.

But for some notable exceptions, the first signs of good or outstanding
intellectual ability can be observed earlier than those of any others,
because it affects everything a baby has to learn. In particular, the able
child tends to learn to talk early and to acquire a large vocabulary
quickly; often he shows an unusual capacity for quick and sustained
attention. Not only is he a quick learner, he also eagerly seeks knowledge
and information. While the popular image pictures him as physically
puny and bespectacled, verbally precocious and a bookworm, emotionally
immature and a poor mixer, such systematic studies as are available
do not support this stereotype. Of course, there is a wide range of
differences in physique, personality, emotional stability and sociability
among both normal and able children. On the whole, however, the
latter are taller, healthier and more advanced physically, emotionally
and socially than their contemporaries. At least, this is the case if things
go reasonably well. What then can be done to ensure that they do so to
a greater extent than at present?

Early identification of ability
In recent years the concept of prevention has come to enjoy increasing
support as a more humane and probably also more economical approach
to children's development. Of course, their basic needs have not changed
and are very similar, whatever the age, ability or handicap. Affection,
security, new experience and recognition of achievement are the
essential prerequisites for human personality development. The differences are considerable when it comes to the exact ways in which these
needs have to be met at different ages and for different groups of children. The outlook today is much more optimistic than it was even
fifteen years ago because of the general acceptance of two facts: first,
the vital influence of the environment in fostering mental abilities while
not denying the role of biological inheritance. The change in outlook
lies in admitting that we do not know the relative importance of nature
and nurture but concentrate on the latter, since—for the time being at
any rate—we can do more about it.

Secondly, there is now a consensus of opinion that it is the pre-school
period which is of fundamental importance to all later development.
In broad terms the areas of agreement cover the vital role of early

learning, be it emotional or intellectual; the crucial part of play and speech for later learning; and the effects of early emotional and intellectual deprivation. The change of outlook lies in the recognition that stimulation or deprivation has pervasive and long-lasting consequences not only in the emotional but also in the intellectual sphere.

The practical implications of these two facts could be quite farreaching if translated into action. In a piecemeal, somewhat patchy, halting and faltering fashion a start has been made in relation to handicapped children. For example, many health authorities keep an 'at risk' register from birth onwards; in some areas babies are screened for phenylketonuria and hearing defects; mentally subnormal children can be ascertained officially from the age of two years onwards; and socially severely disadvantaged children will benefit from the additional nursery schools which are to be provided in educational priority areas.

Though at opposite ends of the scale, very able children are as exceptional as those who are handicapped, both in the strictly numerical sense and in requiring special consideration because of their special needs—though these are less readily appreciated in the case of the able. How and why do these needs arise?

Special needs of the able

For one thing they tend to have interests and concerns well in advance of their actual age. This makes them ask penetrating and profound questions which in the eyes of adults may appear awkward or impudent. Thanks to a good memory and a sensitive perception, they will recall incidents better, brood over inconsistencies and be affronted by expediency and hypocrisy—all of which may make the adults caring for them feel resentful, threatened and unable to cope. Often too they are extremely active, and hence more exhausting to care for, as well as requiring little sleep or objecting to the waste of time this entails. An example of this was recounted by the father of Albert (case study No. 11, p. 44) who as a three-year-old went through a period of refusing to go to sleep, insisting that one of his parents remained in the room. When the father's patience gave way, he slapped him saying 'You must go to sleep', to which Albert replied tearfully: 'I am afraid, I don't know where to go to; tell me.' This left the father baffled, guilty and without a rejoinder.

Even intelligent and educated parents may find a highly able child a difficult challenge. His contemporaries too may avoid his company if he wants to organise their play too much or invent new rules, or if he is usually able to outwit them, do things more quickly or inevitably win. Charles (case study No. 9, p. 38) learned early that to be popular he had to use bribes and that is how his stealing began and eventually culminated in taxi rides and shopping sprees with his awed contemporaries.

Teachers may also find very able children a trial or even a threat, the more inexperienced and insecure the teacher and the younger the child. In such a situation she may fear that her authority is being undermined, together with her precariously maintained authority. Paul (case study No. 12, p. 49) had this effect on his newly qualified teacher in his first term in the infant school. Circumstances were against both of them: they had not hit it off at all, he was already a very disturbed boy with a well-developed passion for numbers, and her weakest point had always been arithmetic. After her first slip on the blackboard, he began to watch like a hawk and delighted in pointing out the slightest error; this in turn demoralised her, giving him more opportunities to show her up.

The opponents of early identification of able children argue that early brightness may be no more than temporary precocity which will not last. This may be true of special talents, such as the writing of poetry or marked skill in drawing or painting. High general ability, in contrast, tends to be constant, though it may be more overtly in evidence at some stages than at others. When some 'fading' does occur it is much more likely that emotional problems are blocking the satisfactory functioning of abilities, or else that the child decided to conceal them in the hope of an easier life.

Another objection might be that it could lead to the expectation of special treatment as of right, intolerance of 'lesser mortals' and an overemphasis of intellectual as against moral, ethical and other equally important qualities, in short, intellectual arrogance. This is a more serious and real problem, to which there is no easy solution. Just as by singling out the handicapped for special attention, the aim is to provide them with fuller opportunities and reduce prejudice against them, so with the very able the aim of education in the fullest sense must be not only to enable them to fulfil their potential abilities but to see these as precious gifts which they are fortunate to possess and which carry with them obligations and responsibilities.

Early identification and action

Early identification of ability does not mean that there is necessarily any action to be taken. It means sounding an alert, being aware that special needs may arise, that greater support, greater tolerance, greater sophistication may be required at certain times and at certain stages. If everything continues to be fairly plain sailing, so much the better.

But the abler the child, the less likely this is to be the case, if for no other reason than that not all aspects of development are likely to be equally advanced. For example, one would not expect a seven-year-old to have the physique of a ten-and-a-half-year-old, even though this was the level of his intellectual ability; and the able five-year-old may be emotionally immature for her age so that there is a wide gap between the way she thinks and the way she feels and behaves. Discrepancies in level of growth create difficulties for all children; to the extent that these are more likely to occur among the able, such children are more vulnerable.

Awareness of a child's good or very exceptional ability will come more readily and will be sharpened by sensitivity to early indicators. Some have already been mentioned, such as early and quick learning, a good memory and a thirst for information and knowledge. Others are the ability to occupy himself and find his own interests; wanting to complete things he has chosen to do; resenting interruption or any interference with his activities and plans; asking questions about fundamental problems such as the meaning of life and death, history or scientific discoveries; pursuing interests beyond his years, in say chess, archaeology or crosswords; persisting with things until he gets them right; being able to laugh at himself and at adult jokes; having unusual sensitivity to other people's feelings and problems. Any one of these, singly or in combination, may be an indication.

Ability—of whatever level or quality—needs nourishment just as the body needs food, if it is to reach its potential height and weight. It is equally essential that the mental 'diet' be right, particularly during the very crucial, earliest years when the child learns how to learn and then during the following years when he has to master the basic tools for more advanced learning by becoming literate and numerate. The wanted and loved child of intelligent and educated parents is fortunate: even though they may not consider him to be very able 'but just like us', they will encourage his growing mind by their response to his curiosity and by making available to him an increasingly challenging range of new experiences; their pleasure at his progress will be the strongest incentive for him to aim at further achievements.

Somewhat less fortunate is the able child whose parents are loving and concerned but look upon early development as a time for 'letting him play and keeping him occupied'. He may well be quite happy but when language remains a serviceable though strictly utilitarian tool, when many of his 'deeper' questions remain inadequately answered and when his curiosity lacks the opportunity to range beyond the ordinary horizon of a child's world—then his mental diet is deficient for an able child. His mind will be undernourished and in time he will become an underachiever. His sights will be set too low and his potential will remain unrealised—unless he is lucky with his teachers.

The need for greater awareness and understanding

How can this situation be avoided? If positive child care and constructive education became more than slogans, then the early identification and promotion of ability would find a place among their aims. Basically these are twofold: to reduce the incidence of intellectual neglect or deprivation; and to reduce the incidence of emotional neglect and deprivation. Or as put positively before, to ensure that children acquire maximal emotional stability so that they are more resilient under the inevitable stresses and strains of life; and to promote the development of all their intellectual and educational potentialities, so that they become fulfilled as individuals and effective as parents and citizens.

Suggestions on how this might be done have been discussed elsewhere[1] and, though the context was different, the same principles and considerations apply. In brief, a much wider dissemination of knowledge and understanding about the various stages of normal child development among school leavers, engaged couples and expectant parents could lead to a greater awareness of how best to meet development needs. This would include an appreciation of individual differences among children as well as insight into the needs not only of the 'normal' child, but also of the handicapped and the able. After all, any one family may well contain one or more of each of these.

Furthermore, advice on children's psychological growth should be as readily available as is guidance on their physical health. This will need a change in the current climate of opinion. There is still a feeling among both parents and teachers that to want advice on emotional or social aspects of a child's growth is either being fussy or a confession of failure. The mass media have contributed to dispelling the fears and prejudice which surround questions of mental health, yet much remains to be done. When it is, the exceptional child will also benefit.

Early detection and enrichment

The mentally 'severely undernourished' child belongs to the unlucky ones who for one reason or another—and frequently there is more than one—receive only minimal stimulation for intellectual and emotional growth: the parents are unable or unwilling to take an interest in his development; they may themselves be semiliterate or illiterate; they

[1] *Investment in Children*, ed. M. L. Kellmer Pringle, Longmans, 1965, chapters 9 and 10.

may be hostile to education; or they may be adequate parents to their other children but have rejected this particular one. Early detection, though essential, is of little avail unless services exist to supplement what is lacking. At best it may mean enriching an impoverished home background, widening the able child's horizons and kindling his curiosity. At worst it may require compensating him for whole areas of missed experiences and attempting to reawaken intellectual curiosity which has been extinguished (Pringle, 1965a).

At present the only places which can provide such enrichment are nursery schools though this is not, of course, their primary purpose. In the past they have always been willing to absorb a proportion of children with mental, physical or social handicaps. Now events are imposing this task on them in educational priority areas and probably also in community development projects in a much more deliberate and intensive way. The methods used in nursery schools are, overall, the most enlightened because they are most adapted to developing the potential of each child; but they may well be neither comprehensive enough nor sufficiently adapted to the special needs of the severely underprivileged and deprived. Simply diluting what is normally done and working at a slower pace is no more likely to succeed than did the watering down of grammar school curricula for slow-learning children. These new demands are bound to present nursery schools with very taxing problems but it is to be hoped they will be able to pay some special attention to what might well be a minority group with additional needs. There is little doubt, too, that in quite a high proportion of cases the parents of the more able child will need case-work help in an endeavour to make the home more supportive to the child and more aware of his needs.

Early diagnosis and treatment of able misfits
Most attempts to evaluate the effectiveness of preventive and treatment programmes indicate better and more lasting results with younger children rather than youth. Yet, here as in so many other fields, diagnosis and treatment tend to be delayed unless underachievement is accompanied by behaviour difficulties of an aggressive type. Going to school may present a second chance to the 'undernourished' able child if he is fortunate enough to attend an informal, unstreamed, family-grouped primary school. But by itself this is not enough. Additionally, he needs a highly perceptive teacher who can observe him over a considerable period so that she becomes sensitive not only to what he does but what he might be able to do. Toby, the handicapped boy described earlier (case study No. 14, p. 56) had just such a teacher: yet even she needed

all the courage of her conviction to persuade the headteacher that she was not simply seeing a swan in her failing duckling. And Toby had loving and accepting parents but even they had not seen, or perhaps had not dared to see, his considerable intellectual potential.

Probably for most 'undernourished' able children, school fails to present this second chance. Under present day conditions this is hardly surprising. Careful and skilled observation of individual children in a class of forty or more infants or juniors is an impossible task for all but the most gifted teacher. And there is no reason to expect a higher proportion of geniuses among the teaching profession than there is among any other. Hence one of two things is likely to happen: the able child whose potential has remained largely dormant may get by, performing at an average or possibly below average level for his age. Or he becomes so bored by methods and curricula geared to the average, that his interest and curiosity are never aroused; consequently he opts out altogether, becoming not only a misfit but a failure. Albert (case study No. 11, p. 44) is an example of this, but he had severe emotional problems too which would probably have been beyond the capacity of any ordinary school.

It is likely that good ability could be detected during the first year in the juniors (that is at the age of seven or eight years) if it has failed to come to light at an earlier stage. In a fully developed and integrated system of early identification, early detection of undernourishment and facilities for enriched or compensatory pre-school provision, the school would play an integral role in the continuous and continuing process of observation, diagnosis and treatment. In the absence of such a system, the primary school is confronted with an even greater responsibility for talent spotting.

Experimental schemes in the USA

How can this be at least attempted? Various schemes are being tried out in the United States. Though their educational system as well as their standards are different, a look at some of these approaches is well worth while, even knowing that both their problems and their resources are on a much vaster scale than ours.

One of the most interesting is the 'Early Identification and Prevention' programme launched in forty-two primary schools in different sections of New York. In contrast to many other schemes it is intended for children of all economic, social and cultural levels. It is based on the belief that obstacles to learning may relate to physical, emotional or social factors, that they may become focused on a particular subject or on all school work, and that there is likely to be a link with later delinquent behaviour, limited vocational aims and early school

leaving. Also that the later any steps are taken to overcome the difficulties, the greater the effort that is needed and the less the chance of
success.

The age of eight to ten years is thought to be a crucial stage at which
vulnerable children get overwhelmed by their difficulties, even if these
are not fully developed by then. Hence the programme begins with
five- to seven-year-olds. Its second distinguishing feature is a team
approach. Each of the forty-two schools is provided with a school
counsellor, a half-time psychologist and a half-time social worker;
psychiatric consultation is available. The team functions co-operatively
with the school staff, with individual children and with their families.
The major part of the work is done through discussions with teachers,
observations of children, individual and group conferences, and semi-
nars with parents and with teachers. Children who are seriously disturbed are given psychiatric treatment.

Another large-scale programme is the 'Talent Preservation Project'
concentrated on fifteen- to seventeen-year-olds, also in New York City
schools. While in the former project, election of children was based
partly on teachers' referrals and partly on firsthand observation by
the teams themselves, here some 2,000 young people were selected by
means of an educational and developmental test battery. A variety of
approaches was used, including additional teaching in particular subjects, group counselling and intensive individual counselling, group
therapy, motivational groups, social workers' interviews with pupils and
with parents.

Though special additional teaching was the most frequent recommendation made by teachers and counsellors, this seemed less effective,
whereas approaches relating to motivational factors made the relatively
greatest impact on academic achievement. This is a particularly interesting finding since results from one of our own longitudinal studies
also led us to the conclusion that 'it may well be that fostering emotional
and social potential may prove more conducive to improving a child's
rate of learning than concentrating more directly, but narrowly, on
educational progress itself' (Gooch and Pringle, 1966).

In 1960 a massive scheme entitled 'Project Talent' was launched as the
'first scientifically planned national inventory of the human talents in
the United States'. It was conducted so as to coincide with the 1960
population census. A selected sample of half a million fourteen- to
seventeen-year-olds was given a two-day series of tests of ability, attainment, interests and personality characteristics. A follow-up is planned
to try to find out how closely the future accomplishments of these young
people is matching their potential as predicted by the test battery.

Currently available tests and measurements

Dissatisfaction has been expressed with the various measures used
hitherto to discover underachievers by group tests, largely because
these have leaned too heavily on convergent or conventional, rather
than divergent or creative thinking. Also it is felt that a greater variety
of measures needs to be developed so that motivation and values can
be explored as well as interests. The same criticisms apply to most test
batteries used in this country to discover underachievers. Certainly in
the short run, but probably also in the long, teachers' observations and
judgments as well as parents' anxieties about their children's potential
and actual performance will remain the basic tools for initiating screening procedures to discover the able misfit. Nor must the effect of the
concerned teacher coupled with the conviction that a pupil has much
greater potential than is apparent be underrated. Recent research has
shown not only that the achievement of those pupils of whom little is
expected becomes progressively less, but also that those from whom the
teacher is led to expect more do in fact produce better work. This is
not saying that unrealistically high expectations and pressure to come
up to them is a useful approach in the absence of a child's ability to
improve his rate of learning. Rather this finding pinpoints the contribution made to progress by a teacher's optimistic or pessimistic frame of
mind. As our case studies showed (Nos. 1 to 6, pp. 12–33) too high
parental expectation had the very opposite effect from that intended,
despite the children's undoubtedly good ability and their teachers'
dissatisfaction with their achievements.

Conclusions

CAUSE FOR CONCERN

There is much evidence—in the literature of psychology, education and
manpower problems—of the existence of a sizeable degree of under-
development or underutilisation of human ability. The present position
of how and where abilities are lost, can be summarised in this way:
children who fail to be identified as possessing good ability, often will
not receive appropriate educational stimulation and opportunity. Inci-
dentally, available measuring instruments leave much to be desired.
Such underachievement occurs more frequently among children who
have emotional problems, who come from low income, and probably
also from immigrant, families. They tend to leave school at the earliest
opportunity. Underutilisation at this stage is particularly marked
among girls. Not only does any comparative superiority, shown during
the earlier school years, gradually disappear but a much smaller proportion go on to tertiary education.

For example, while 90 per cent of pupils from professional homes passed in at least three subjects at GCE O level, among those whose fathers were doing unskilled work only 46 per cent did so, yet all of them had obtained excellent marks in the 11-plus selection examination (Furneaux, 1961). In colleges and universities this waste of ability continues: considering how extremely competitive entry to such institutions is and how high the cost per place, it is remarkable that the subsequent failure rate arouses so little concern.

FACTORS CONDUCIVE TO ACHIEVEMENT

Among the most important ones are parental interest in their child's development and attitudes towards education; the quality of education available wherever the family happens to live; the conscious and unconscious motivation of the children in relation to learning and achievement; the availability of an admired and achieving adult with whom they can identify; the availability and quality of guidance and remedial services; community and particularly neighbourhood attitudes towards education; and the attitudes of teachers and administrators towards children.

IMPROVING DETECTION TECHNIQUES

Because high ability is a complex phenomenon, there is a need to develop more complex diagnostic measures than have been used hitherto. In addition to tests of intellect, they must include personality variables, such as motivation and self-concepts as well as creativity and specific abilities. For example, relatively unsophisticated projective material has been found to contain promising features which suggests that they might become useful screening devices in the hands of teachers with a special interest and training in this field (Gooch and Pringle, 1966). Also it looks as if there are stages in personal–social development which can be detected by such projective tasks and which are related both to attainment level and to the rate of progress over the years.

Better long-term criteria for success will have to be developed in terms of adult work performance and satisfaction; short-term and intermediate range criteria also require considerable further development so as to go beyond mere scholastic achievement, which until now has remained the keystone of identification methods.

'True, a man has to go to school to become a pilot, a doctor or a statesman; but it is not safe to use school aptitude alone as a means for weeding out the unfit—unless one is certain that scholastic aptitude is requiring the same thing of a man as the job itself will require. . . . In a mobile society like ours, where it is difficult to predict what

values, abilities and motives may be required of a man, it might be
better strategy to develop measures which relate moderately well to
several criteria' (McClelland, 1958).

How to do so early enough, is perhaps the crux of the whole matter.
The challenge lies not so much in recognising ability after it has revealed
itself, but in identifying it when it is largely an unexpressed potential.
Only then can the next step be taken, the provision of an environment
and education which facilitate its development and fulfilment. Of
course, identification of the really able is an integral part of the good
school's effort to understand and cater for individual differences among
all its pupils, providing appropriate learning experiences according to
the 'age, ability and aptitude' of each. It is the gulf between the best
and the worst that needs narrowing.

POSSIBLE REMEDIES
In this country, no large scale efforts have been made either to identify
or to remedy underachievement among able children. In the United
States various schemes have been introduced: some have aimed at
providing more personal, academic and vocational counselling; others
have concentrated on adapting the curriculum, including the moderni-
sation of teaching methods and subject matter; still others have introduced remedial or enrichment programmes; and in some areas, these
approaches have been combined in various ways.

One common feature which has emerged from all these efforts is
'the stubbornness of underachievement'. It is deep-seated and cumulative in nature and, because it is steeped in community and subcultural
influences, it cannot be solved by the school alone. Thus remedies are
likely to succeed only if they are equally complex and comprehensive
to encompass the many facets and characteristics of the problem.

No environment guarantees high achievement or consigns its pupils
irrevocably to low achievement. But a much higher proportion of
children with unrealised potential will be found among certain economic
sectors, social classes, ethnic groups and geographic areas than in others.
The best schools are not only alive to these problems but need to be
enabled by administrators to put a greater wealth of teaching materials,
supporting remedial services and other resources at the disposal of its
teachers.

Teachers themselves often exert the strongest and most lasting
influence on their pupils through their own personalities. This aspect
is particularly important for those able children who lack appropriate
model figures in their own family. Underachievers have been shown to

perform better with supportive, encouraging teachers than with those who simply demand high standards of work.

Among the remedies, improving the self-concept and morale of the underachiever and enlisting parental interest and support occupy pride of place. Community, neighbourhood and peer group attitudes towards intellectual achievement may also need modifying, but this is inevitably a long-term goal. In school, the opportunity to work independently, to explore individual interests in depth, to develop or perhaps rediscover a sense of commitment and excitement about learning—all these are prerequisites for rehabilitating the able misfit.

At present it seems an overwhelming task to provide educational experiences which are, as it were, tailormade for each individual child. With increased knowledge, both about the ways in which different children learn and the different approaches particularly suited to these ways, this task is likely to become less formidable. Torrance suggested an analogy which he believes to be useful in understanding at least two different types of learners (Torrance and Strom, 1965). It comes from his experience of training pets.

To begin with he had dogs and found that they would become reasonably well-behaved, affectionate and loyal pets, if undesirable behaviour was punished and desirable behaviour rewarded. Subsequently when he applied the same training methods to cats, he failed dismally. Eventually he came to understand that there are fundamental differences in the ways by which cats and dogs learn; dogs tend to learn by authority and they are anxious to please; cats learn creatively, by exploring, searching and manipulating. Of course, dogs too are curious and learn in creative ways while cats also respond to firm limits and deliberate methods; the big difference is in preferred ways of learning.

Torrance argues that the able child, like the cat, needs a responsive environment rather than a stimulating one. A responsive environment is seen as being quite different from a 'permissive atmosphere'. It requires alert and sensitive guidance and direction; the ability to listen, observe and encourage; and a willingness to avoid deflecting the child's thinking processes from possibly unconventional channels. Many less able children, though certainly not all, benefit from being provided with a stimulating environment and they prefer to learn by authority.

Underachievement, like envy, seems to feed on itself. A poor start soon snowballs into chronic failure and the teacher's understandable disappointment in poor progress only serves to lead to further discouragement in the pupil. And so both are caught in the vicious circle of discouragement, disapproval, unresponsiveness and further failure. There is no other solution than, and no short cut to, the need for a continuous programme of early identification, early guidance and early attempts to apply more prolonged and complex remedies once the simpler ones have proved ineffective.

There is a temptation to argue that we cannot afford to divert scarce resources of manpower—teachers, psychologists and social workers—to give increasing attention to able misfits, when there are so many under-functioning children who are culturally and socially underprivileged. But in a very real sense this is simply the reverse side of the coin. Just because demands for educated manpower exceed supply, it is essential that underdeveloped but potential intellectual resources be detected and fostered.

At the same time it must be recognised that vastly improved diagnostic and remedial provision will not become available in the immediate future, nor can such services be developed quickly; if for no other reason, because of the lengthy training required by the professional staff. Therefore the responsibility for detecting and fostering the potential of able children will continue to be primarily that of teachers and parents. Hence much more need be done than is the case at present, to arouse among parents and teachers an interest in and concern for able under-achievers. This in turn has implications for teacher training, for in-service refresher courses and for parent–teacher co-operation. The mass media, too, could play an important part in bringing the problem to the public's attention.

Recent years have seen a conflict of viewpoint between those who argue that everyone must be given an equal educational chance and those who advocate that special attention must be given to the very able child. The former make a case for positive discrimination in favour of the socially and culturally disadvantaged child; whereas the latter claim that the nation's ability to compete successfully in a scientific and technological age depends on the fostering of excellence. On reflection the conflict between these two standpoints is more apparent than real. It springs from the mistaken belief that all men are equal despite the enormous disparity found in physical and intellectual potential in all walks of life. To be given equality of opportunity is the right of every child; to expect equal capacity to make use of this opportunity runs counter to common sense and experience. In fact, it has harmful consequences because such expectation is bound to engender a sense of failure.

Instead, we must act *as if* all men were equal and then respect, as well as accept and cater for, their differences. Within such a framework it is legitimate to strive for excellence so that we provide a democracy of opportunity while at the same time ensuring an aristocracy of achievement.

There is one man in this country who over the past fifty years has done more than any other to draw attention to the needs of the backward as well as of the able child both in his writing and in his researches. So it is appropriate to let his be the last word.

'In spite of popular prejudice there is, or there should be, no insuperable conflict between equality as a principle of justice and inequality as a fact of genetics. In education equal opportunity means equal opportunity to make the most of differences that are innate. The ideal is a free and fair chance to each individual, not to rise to the same rank in life as everyone else, but to develop the peculiar gifts and virtues with which he is endowed—high ability if he possesses it, if not, whatever qualities of body, mind, and character are latent within him. In this way, and this way alone, can we be sure of realising to the full our untapped resources of talent, and warding off the decline and fall that has in the end overtaken each of the great civilisations of the past' (Burt, 1962).

APPENDIX
Tables 1-38

Appendix : Tables 1–38

Table 1. Sources of referral

	N	School	Parent	Doctor*	Education Officer	Probation Officer
Boys	75	46	10	7	7	5
Girls	28	20	6	2	—	—
Both	103	66	16	9	7	5

* This includes School Medical Officers, G.P.s, psychiatrists, and other specialists.

Table 2. Type of school attended at time of referral

	N	Pre-school	PRIMARY State	Private	SECONDARY Grammar	Modern	Private
Boys	75	—	48	7	12	6	2
Girls	28	1	9	3	11	—	4
Both	103	1	57	10	23	6	6

Table 3. Reasons for referral

	N	Educational difficulties N	%	Behaviour problems N	%	Both N	%	Physical handicap N	%	Other difficulties N	%
Boys	75	60	80	28	37	13	17	3	4	16	21
Girls	28	27	96	10	36	9	34	1	4	4	14
Both	103	87	84	38	36	22	21	4	4	20	20

Table 4. Nature of Educational Difficulties

	N	All School work N	%	Reading N	%	Spelling N	%	English N	%	Hand-writing N	%	Arith-metic N	%	Others N	%
Boys	60	26	43	13	22	10	17	6	10	2	3	13	22	14	23
Girls	27	13	48	3	11	7	26	3	11	—	—	6	22	2	27
Both	87	39	45	16	18	17	20	9	10	2	2	19	22	16	18

Table 5. Chronological age, mental age and intelligence quotients*

N = 103; 75 boys and 28 girls

	C.A. AT REFERRAL Mean yr mth	Range yr mth to yr mth	M.A. Mean yr mth	Range yr mth to yr mth	I.Q. yr mth Mean	Range
Boys	10 0	5 11 to 16 5	13 6	8 11 to 21 10	134·8	120 to 208
Girls	11 5	4 6 to 17 10	14 11	6 6 to 20 9	131·3	120 to 149
Both	10 5	4 6 to 17 10	13 11	6 6 to 21 10	133·8	120 to 208

* All the above results refer to Terman Merrill I.Q.s (using the Roberts-Mellone correction where applicable), except for six children. Because of their ages, the WISC was used for three of them and the WAIS for the other three cases.

Table 6. Age distribution

N = 103; 75 boys and 28 girls

	4 yr 11 mth and below N	%	5 yr to 6 yr 11 mth N	%	7 yr to 10 yr 11 mth N	%	11 yr to 14 yr 11 mth N	%	15 yr and above N	%
Boys	—	—	3	4	51	68	16	21	5	7
Girls	2	7	2	7	8	29	9	32	7	25
Both	2	2	5	5	59	58	25	24	12	11

Table 7. I.Q. distribution

I.Q. range	%
120 to 139	78
140 to 159	17
160 to 179	4
180 and above	1

Table 8. Attainment in reading
N = 77; 61 boys and 16 girls

	C.A. Mean		C.A. Range				R.A. Mean		R.A. Range				M.A. Mean		M.A. Range			
	yr	mth	yr	mth	yr	mth	yr	mth	yr	mth	yr	mth	yr	mth	yr	mth	yr	mth
Boys	9	9	5	11 to	16	4	9	11	5	1 to	15	0	12	0	8	11 to	19	5
Girls	10	5	5	0 to	17	3	11	1	5	4 to	14	11	13	8	7	4 to	20	9
Both	9	11	5	0 to	17	3	10	2	5	1 to	15	0	13	0	7	4 to	20	9

Table 9. Attainment in spelling
N = 48; 35 boys and 12 girls

	C.A. Mean		C.A. Range				S.A. Mean		S.A. Range				M.A. Mean		M.A. Range			
	yr	mth	yr	mth	yr	mth	yr	mth	yr	mth	yr	mth	yr	mth	yr	mth	yr	mth
Boys	9	9	5	11 to	16	4	8	9	5	3 to	12	5	12	10	10	2 to	19	0
Girls	11	10	5	8 to	17	3	10	6	7	2 to	14	9	15	7	10	4 to	20	9
Both	10	4	5	11 to	17	3	9	2	5	3 to	14	9	13	7	10	2 to	20	9

Table 10. Attainment in arithmetic

N = 51; 44 boys and 7 girls

| | C.A. | | A.A. | | M.A. | |
| | Mean | Range | Mean | Range | Mean | Range |
	yr mth	yr mth yr mth	yr mth	yr mth yr mth	yr mth	yr mth yr mth
Boys	10 4	7 2 to 16 5	10 4	7 1 to 17 0	13 10	10 6 to 20 1
Girls	11 3	9 5 to 13 5	11 1	8 6 to 15 0	15 0	12 0 to 19 1
Both	10 6	7 2 to 16 5	10 5	8 6 to 17 0	14 0	10 6 to 20 1

Table 11. Degree of backwardness and underachievement in the basic subjects

Subject	12–23 mth below C.A.		2 yr or more below C.A.		2 yr or more below M.A.	
	N	%	N	%	N	%
Reading N = 77	25	32	16	21	53	69
Spelling N = 48	12	24	14	29	44	92
Arithmetic N = 51	26	51	4	8	39	76
Two or more subjects N = 89	41	46	23	26	75	84

Table 12. Predominant type of difficulty found at the diagnostic examination
N = 103; 75 boys and 28 girls

	Learning difficulties without behaviour difficulties		Learning difficulties with some behaviour difficulties		Behaviour difficulties with some learning difficulties	
	N	%	N	%	N	%
Boys	14	19	47	62	14	19
Girls	7	25	16	57	5	18
Both	21	20	63	61	19	19

Table 13. Distribution of behaviour patterns
N = 103; 75 boys and 28 girls

	Normal		Anxious		Withdrawn		Aggressive		Mixed	
	N	%	N	%	N	%	N	%	N	%
Boys	14	19	14	19	17	23	11	14	19	25
Girls	4	14	14	50	5	18	5	18	—	—
Both	18	18	28	27	22	21	16	16	19	18

Table 14. Average number of symptoms

	Nervous	Habit disorders	Behaviour disorders	All
Boys	1·9	0·5	1·8	4·2
Girls	1·6	0·3	1·1	3·1
Both	1·8	0·5	1·6	3·9

Table 15. Average number of symptoms in relation to behaviour patterns
N = 103; 75 boys and 28 girls

| | BEHAVIOUR PATTERN | | | | |
Symptoms	Normal N = 18	Anxious N = 28	Withdrawn N = 22	Aggressive N = 16	Mixed N = 19
Nervous	0·2	2·1	3·5	0·6	2·1
Habit disorders	0·1	0·3	0·8	0·2	1·0
Behaviour disorders	0·3	0·6	1·0	4·0	2·8
All	0·61	3·07	5·36	4·75	5·84

Table 16. Percentage distribution of symptoms within each behaviour pattern
N = 103

| | BEHAVIOUR PATTERN | | | | |
Symptoms	Anxious N = 28	Withdrawn N = 22	Aggressive N = 16	Mixed N = 19	Total
Nervous	69	66	12	35	47
Habit disorders	10	15	4	17	13
Behaviour disorders	21	19	84	48	40

Table 17. Level of social competence
N = 50; 41 boys and 9 girls

	C.A. Mean		M.A. Mean		I.Q. Mean	S.A. Mean		S.Q. Range	S.Q. Mean
	yr	mth	yr	mth		yr	mth		
Boys	9	7	13	2	134·3	9	0	72 to 109	94·2
Girls	9	1	12	1	131·6	8	3	79 to 95	90·6
Both	9	6	13	0	133·8	8	10	72 109	93·5

Table 18. Relationship of no. of symptoms with educational retardation

	None, one or two symptoms	Three or more symptoms
	N = 50; 33b and 17g	N = 53; 42b and 11g
Mean C.A.	10 yr, 11 mth	10 yr, 3 mth
Mean I.Q.	133·52	132·98
% retarded in reading	48	55
% retarded in spelling	38	47
% retarded in arithmetic	32	43
% retarded in one or more subjects	68	77

Table 19. Type and no. of symptoms for 'better' readers and 'better' arithmeticians

Symptoms	Reading better N = 11	Arithmetic better N = 10
Nervous symptoms	27	14
Habit disorders	7	4
Behaviour disorders	20	11
Average no. of symptoms per child	4·9	2·9

Table 20. Fathers' occupational status and mothers working (percentages)

	FATHERS' OCCUPATIONAL STATUS			MOTHERS' WORKING		
	Profess. and Managerial	Non-Manual	Skilled, semi-and unskilled	Part-time	Full-time	At home
Boys	47	25	28	20	12	68
Girls	44	30	26	30	7	63
Both	46	27	27	22	11	67

Table 21. Parents' education (percentages)

	Elementary left at 14	Grammar/technical	Private/boarding	Commercial/evening course	University	Profess. training
Fathers	43	50	6	5	12	4
Mothers	57	28	15	7	6	5

Table 22. Living conditions of referral (percentages)

	House				Flat	Over business premises
	Rented	Owned	Owned but relatives living with family	Family living in house of relatives		
All children	22	53	14	6	3	2

Table 23. Position in family
N = 103; 75 boys and 28 girls (percentages)

	Only	Oldest	Middle	Youngest
Boys	21	39	9	31
Girls	43	21	15	21
Both	27	35	10	28

Table 24. Position in family of children referred because of behaviour difficulties (percentages)
N = 38: 27 boys and 11 girls

Oldest	Only	Youngest	Middle
45	26	24	5

Table 25. Position in family in relation to child's behaviour pattern (percentages)
N = 103

	BEHAVIOUR PATTERN				
	Normal	Anxious	With-drawn	Aggres-sive	Mixed
First-born (N = 63)	12	21	29	19	19
The rest (N = 40)	24	38	10	10	18

Table 26. Cultural stimulation in the home and child's interests (percentages)
N = 103; 75 boys and 28 girls

		Above average	Average	Below average
Cultural stimulation	Boys	38	24	38
	Girls	14	38	48
	Both	32	28	40
Newspapers	Boys	44	21	35
	Girls	24	41	35
	Both	38	27	35
Child's interests	Boys	19	36	45
	Girls	14	48	38
	Both	18	39	43

Table 27. Cultural stimulation and child's interests in relation to father's occupational status (percentages)
N = 103

	Father's occupation	Above average	Average	Below average
Cultural stimulation	Profess./			
	Managerial	56	23	21
	Non-manual	21	33	46
	Skilled/			
	unskilled	—	30	70
Newspapers	Profess./			
	Managerial	67	7	26
	Non-manual	26	32	42
	Skilled/			
	unskilled	—	57	43
Child's interests	Profess./			
	Managerial	21	33	46
	Non-manual	19	48	33
	Skilled/			
	unskilled	16	47	37

Table 28. Opportunities for independence and social contacts (percentages)
N = 103

		Above average	Average	Below average
Opportunities for	Boys	18	33	49
independence	Girls	6	44	50
	Both	15	36	49
Social contact—pre-school	Boys	8	21	71
	Girls	—	33	67
	Both	6	24	70
Social contact—school age	Boys	6	42	52
	Girls	9	30	61
	Both	7	38	55

Table 29. Opportunities for independence and social contacts in relation to fathers' occupational status (percentages)
N = 103

	Father's occupation	Above average	Average	Below average
Opportunities for independence	Profess./ Managerial	15	35	50
	Non-manual	22	39	39
	Skilled/ unskilled	6	38	56
Social contact— pre-school	Profess./ Managerial	3	3	94
	Non-manual	8	50	42
	Skilled/ unskilled	11	28	61
Social contact— school age	Profess./ Managerial	2	28	70
	Non-manual	9	67	24
	Skilled/ unskilled	13	39	48

Table 30. Child's behaviour pattern in relation to home atmosphere (percentages)
N = 103

Home atmosphere	BEHAVIOUR PATTERN				
	Normal	Anxious	Withdrawn	Aggressive	Mixed
Harmonious	75	12	7	6	—
Fair	16	22	28	14	20
Unfavourable	8	32	18	22	20

Table 31. Parental discipline (percentages)
N = 103

	Sensible	Strict	Indulgent	Inconsistent
Boys	25	9	26	40
Girls	29	25	17	29
Both	26	13	24	37

Table 32. Discipline in relation to fathers' occupational status (percentages)
N = 103

Father's occupation	Sensible	Strict	Indulgent	Inconsistent
Profess./Managerial	23	16	19	42
Non-manual	42	4	25	29
Skilled/unskilled	17	17	36	30

Table 33. Child's behaviour pattern in relation to parental discipline (percentages)
N = 103

Parental discipline	BEHAVIOUR PATTERN				
	Normal	Anxious	Withdrawn	Aggressive	Mixed
Sensible	70	16	5	5	4
Strict	17	42	14	27	—
Indulgent	10	17	41	8	24
Inconsistent	8	15	11	28	38

Table 34. Parental attitudes to child's educational progress (percentages)
N = 103; 75 boys and 28 girls

	Normal interest	Concerned	Over-anxious	Indifferent
Boys	21	38	37	4
Girls	32	25	43	—
Both	24	34	40	2

Table 35. Parental attitudes to child's emotional development (percentages)
N = 103; 75 boys and 28 girls

	Normal interest	Concerned	Over-anxious	Indifferent
Boys	27	18	24	31
Girls	36	25	18	21
Both	30	20	22	28

Table 36. Parental attitudes to child's educational progress in relation to father's occupational status (percentages)
N = 103

Father's occupation	PARENTAL ATTITUDES			
	Normal interest	Concerned	Over-anxious	Indifferent
Profess./Managerial	11	30	59	—
Non-manual	38	47	15	—
Skilled/unskilled	33	26	30	11

Table 37. Parental attitudes to child's emotional development in relation to fathers' occupational status (percentages)
N = 103

	PARENTAL ATTITUDES			
Father's occupation	Normal interest	Concerned	Over-anxious	Indifferent
Profess./Managerial	33	13	28	26
Non-manual	36	35	11	18
Skilled/unskilled	22	22	22	34

Table 38. Recommendation made (percentages)
N = 103; 75 boys and 28 girls

	Attend Dept.	ADVICE		EDUC. CHANGE		Medical exam.	Re-test	Private Tuition
		Parents	School	Stream	School			
Boys	61	40	13	4	17	19	12	7
Girls	64	39	7	—	25	7	7	4
Both	62	40	12	3	19	16	11	6

Bibliography

ARMSTRONG, H. G. (1967) 'Wastage of ability amongst the intellectually gifted,' *Brit. J. Ed. Psychol.*, **37**, No. 2, 257-9.

AUSUBEL, D. P. (1951) 'Prestige motivation of gifted children,' *Genet. Psychol. Mon.*, **43**, 53-117.

BALDWIN, A. L., KALHOUN, J. and BREESE, F. H. (1945) 'Patterns of parent behaviour', *Psychol. Mon.*, **58**, no. 3, whole no. 268.

BARBE, W. B. (1956a) 'Problems in reading encountered by gifted children', *Elementary English*, **33**, 274-8.

BARBE, W. B. (1956b) 'A study of the family background of the gifted', *J. Ed. Psychol.*, **47**, 302-9.

BARRETT, H. O. (1957) 'An intensive study of 32 gifted children', *Personnel and Guid. Journal*, **36**, 192-4.

BEASLEY, J. (1957) *Underachievement; Review of the Literature* (Talented Youth Project of the Horace Mann-Lincoln Inst. of School Experimentation.) Teachers' College, Columbia University.

BEREDAY, G. Z. F. and LAUWERYS, J. A. (1962) 'The gifted child', *Yearbook of Education*, Evans.

BERMAN, A. B. and KLEIN, A. (1942) 'Personality study of maladjusted pupils of superior mentality', *High Points*, **24**, 57-63.

BISHTON, R. C. (1956) 'Study of some factors related to achievement of intellectually superior eighth-grade children', *Dissertation Abstr.*, **16**, 64-5.

BOARDMAN, R. K. and HILDRETH, G. H. (1948) 'Adjustment problems of the gifted', *Understanding children*, **17**, 41-4, 51.

BONSALL, M. R. and STEFFLRE, B. (1960) 'The temperament of gifted children', in *Educating the Gifted* (ed. J. L. French). Holt & Co.

ED BRIDGES, S. A. (1969) *Gifted Children and the Brentwood Experiment.* Sir Isaac Pitman and Sons.

BRIDGMAN, D. S. (1960) 'Where the loss of talent occurs and why', in *The Search for Talent*, College Entrance Examination Board, New York.

BROWN, A. W. (1926) *Unevenness of the Abilities of Dull and Bright Children* (Contributions to Education, No. 220). Teachers' College, Columbia University.

BURNS, C. L. C. (1949) 'Maladjusted children of high intelligence', *Brit. J. ed. Psychol.*, **19**, 137-41.

BURNSIDE, L. H. (July–Aug. 1942) 'Psychological guidance of gifted children', *J. consult. Psychol.*, **6**, 223-8.

BURT, Sir C. (1947) *Mental and Scholastic Tests*, Staples Press.

BURT, Sir C. (1961) 'The gifted child', *Brit. J. stat. Psychol.*, **14**, no. 2, 123-39.

BURT, Sir C. (1962a) 'The gifted child', *The Times Educ. Suppl.*, 26 Jan.

BURT, Sir C. (1962b) 'The gifted child', in *Year Book of Education*, General Introduction, pp. 24-58. Evans.

BUTLER, N. R. and ALBERMAN, E. (1968) *Perinatal Problems*. Livingstone.

BUTLER, N. R. and BONHAM, D. G. (1964) *Perinatal Mortality*. Livingstone.

CARLSON, E. F. (1944) 'Problems in education of the highly endowed', *Childhood Education* (March issue).

CARROLL, H. A. (1940) 'Intellectually gifted children; their characteristics and problems', *Teachers' Coll. Rec.*, **42**, 212-27.

CHAZAN, M. (1959) 'Maladjusted children in grammar schools', *Brit. J. ed. Psychol.*, **29**, no. 3, 198-206.

CICIRELLI, V. G. (1967) 'Sibling constellation, creativity, I.Q. and academic achievement', *Child Development*, **38**, no. 2. Univ. Chicago Press.

CONKLIN, A. M. (1940) *Failures of Highly Intelligent Pupils*. Bureau of Publications, Teachers' Coll. Columbia Univ.

CROWDER, T. and GALLAGHER, J. J. (1957) 'Adjustment of gifted children in the regular classroom: Case studies', *Except. Child.*, **23**, 353-63, 396-8.

CUTTS, N. E. and MOSELEY, N. (1957) *Teaching the Bright and Gifted*. Prentice-Hall.

DAVIDS, A. and SIDMAN, J. (1962) 'A pilot study—impulsivity, time orientation, and delayed gratification in future scientists and in underachieving high school students', *Except Child.*, **29**, no. 4, 170-4.

DAVIS, D. R. and KENT, N. (1955) 'Psychological factors in educational disability', *Proc. Roy. Soc. Med.*, **48**, 993-5.

DE HAAN, R. F. and HAVIGHURST, R. J. (1957) *Educating Gifted Children*. Univ. Chicago Press.

D'HEURLE, E. A., MELLINGER, J. C. and HAGGARD, E. A. (1959) 'Personality, intellectual and achievement patterns in gifted children', *Psychol. Mon.*, **73**, no. 13 (whole no. 483).

DINNAGE, R. and PRINGLE, M. L. KELLMER (1967) *Foster Care-Facts and Fallacies*, Longmans in association with the National Bureau for Co-operation in Child Care.

DOUGLAS, J. W. B. (1964) *The Home and the School*. MacGibbon and Kee.

DOUGLAS, J. W. B., ROSS, J. M. and SIMPSON, H. R. (1968) *All our Future*. Peter Davies.

DOWD, R. J. (June, 1952) 'Underachieving students of high capacity', *J. Higher Educ.*, **23**, 327-30.

DREWS, E. M. (1962) 'Realisation of talent among children', in Bereday and Lauwerys, 1962.

DREWS, E. M. and TEAHAN, J. E. (1957) 'Parental attitudes and academic achievement', *J. clin. Psychol.*, **13**, 328-32.

DUFF, J. F. (1929) 'Children of high intelligence, a follow up enquiry', *Brit. J. Psychol.*, **19**, 413-38.

DURR, W. K. (1960) 'Characteristics of gifted children: ten years of research', *The Gifted Child Quarterly*, **4**, no. 4, 75-9.

EDELSTON, H. (1950) 'Educational failure with high intelligence quotient; a clinical study', *J. Genet. Psychol.*, **77**, 85-116.

FLANAGAN, J. C. and BAILEY, J. T. (1960) 'Project talent—the identification, development and utilization of human talents', *Personnel and Guidance Journal*, 504-5.

FLIEGLER, L. A. (1957) 'Understanding the underachieving gifted child', *Psychol. Rep.*, **3**, 533-6.

FLOUD, J. E., HALSEY, A. H. and MARTIN, F. M. (1957) *Social Class and Educational Opportunity*. Heinemann.

FRANKEL, E. (1960) 'A comparative study of achieving and underachieving high school boys of high intellectual ability', *J. educ. Res.*, **53**, 172-80.

FRENCH, J. L., ed. (1959) *Educating the Gifted, a book of readings*. Holt & Co.

FURNEAUX, W. D. (1961) *The Chosen Few*. Oxford University Press.

GALLAGHER, J. J. and CROWDER, T. (1957) 'The adjustment of gifted children in the regular classroom', *Except. Child.*, **23**, 306-12, 317-19.

GALLAGHER, J. J. and ROGGE, W. (1966) 'The gifted', *Rev. ed. Res.*, **36**, no. 1, 37-55.

GOERTZEL, V. and GOERTZEL, M. (1965) *Cradles of Eminence*. Constable.

GOLD, M. J. (1965) *The Education of the Intellectually Gifted Child*. Columbus, Ohio, Charles E. Merrill Books.

GOLDBERG, M. L. and others (1962) 'A three year experimental programme at De Witt High School to help bright under-achievers', in *Readings on the Exceptional Child*, Chap. 21 (eds. E. P. Trapp and P. Himelstein). Methuen.

GOOCH, S. and PRINGLE, M. L. KELLMER (1966) *Four Years On.* Longmans and the National Bureau for Co-operation in Child Care.

GOWAN, J. C. (1952) 'The analysis of leadership in a military school'. Unpublished dissertation, reported in *Psychology and Education of the Gifted* (ed. W. B. Barbe).

GOWAN, J. C. (1955) 'The under-achieving gifted child; a problem for everyone', *Except. Child.*, **21**, 247-9.

GOWAN, J. C. (1957) 'Dynamics of the under-achievement of gifted students', *Except. Child.*, **24**, 98-107.

GREENE, M. M. (1963) 'Overachieving and underachieving gifted high school girls', in *Educating the Academically Able,* Chap. 7 (eds. L. D. Crow and A. Crow), N.Y., McKay.

HAGGARD, E. A. (1957) 'Socialization, personality and academic achievement in gifted children', *Sch. Review,* **65**, 388-414.

HARRIS, C. and TROLTA, F. (1962) 'An experiment with underachievers', *Education,* **82**, 347-9.

HAVIGHURST, R. J. (1962) 'Increasing the pool of talent', in Bereday and Lauwerys, 1962.

HAVIGHURST, R. J., STEVENS, E. and DE HAAN, R. F. (1955) *A Survey of the Education of Gifted Children.* Suppl. Educ. Monograph, No. 83, Univ. Chicago Press.

HOLLINGWORTH, L. S. and TAYLOR, G. A. (1924) 'Size and strength of children who test above 135 I.Q. Studies of physical conditions and growth', *23rd Yearbook,* Nat. Soc. Study Educ., Part I, 221-37.

HOLLINGWORTH, L. S. (1942) *Children Above 140 I.Q.* N.Y., World Book Co.

HORRALL, B. M. (1949) 'Relationship between college aptitude and discouragement buoyancy among college freshmen', *J. Genet. Psychol.*, **74**, 185-243.

HORRALL, B. M. (1957) 'Academic performance and personality adjustment of highly intelligent college students', *Gent. Psychol. Mon.*, **55**, 3-83.

JUSTMAN, J. (1960) 'Some unmet problems in the education of the gifted', *Except. Child.*, **26**, 436-41.

KARNES, M. B. and others (1961) 'Factors associated with under-achievement and over-achievement of intellectually gifted children', *Except. Child.*, **27**, 167-75.

KARNES, M. B. and others (1963) 'The efficacy of two organizational plans for under-achieving gifted children'. *Except. Child.*, **29**, 438-46.

KEPPERS, G. L. and CAPLAN, S. W. (1962) 'Group counselling with academically able underachieving students', New Mexico Studies in Education, *Educ. Res. Bull.* **1**, 12-17.

KIMBALL, B. (1953) 'Case studies in educational failure during adolescence', *Amer. J. Orthopsychiatry*, **23**, 406-15.

KIRK, S. A. and WEINER, B. B. eds. (1963) *Behavioural Research on Exceptional Children*. Council for Exceptional Children, Washington, D.C.

KRUGMAN, M. (1960) 'Identification and preservation of talent', *Teach. Coll. Rec.*, **51**, 459-63.

LAMSON, E. E. (1930) *A Study of Young Gifted Children at Senior High School*. Teachers' Coll., Columbia University.

LANDSTROM, F. M. and NATVIG, A. M. (1954) 'Biographical study of gifted achievers and non-achievers compared with over-achievers and central groups'. Unpublished paper, reported in *Psychology and Education of the Gifted* (ed. W. B. Barbe).

LAYCOCK, S. R. (1933) 'Adjustments of superior and inferior school children', *J. social Psychol.*, **4**, 353-66.

LEWIS, W. D. (1941) 'A comparative study of the personalities, interests and home backgrounds of gifted children of superior and inferior educational achievement', *J. Genet. Psychol.*, **59**, 207-18, Murray State Teachers' College, Kentucky.

LEWIS, W. D. (1943) 'Some characteristics of very superior children', *J. Genet. Psychol.*, **62**, 301-9.

LYNN, R. (1955) 'Temperamental characteristics related to disparity of attainment in reading and arithmetic', *Brit. J. educ. Psychol.*, **27**, 62-7.

LYNN, R. (1959) 'Two personality characteristics related to academic achievement', *Brit. J. educ. Psychol.*, **29**, 213-16

McCLELLAND, D. C. (1955) *Studies in Motivation*. Appleton-Century-Crofts.

McCLELLAND, D. C. (1958) *Issues in the Identification of Talent*. Van Nostrand.

McCLELLAND, D. C., ATKINSON, J. W., CLARK, R. A. and LOWELL, E. L. (1953) *The Achievement Motive*. Appleton-Century-Crofts.

McGILLIVRAY, R. H. (1964) 'Differences in home background between high-achieving and low-achieving gifted children', *Ontario J. ed. Res.*, **6**, no. 2, 99-106.

McLAREN, V. M. (1949) 'Retardation in children of high intelligence', unpublished Ph.D. thesis, Glasgow.

MARTENS, E. H. and others (1933) 'Teachers' problems with exceptional children', in *Gifted Children*, U.S. Office of Education Pamphlet, 41.

MARTINSON, R. A. (1966) 'Issues in the identification of the gifted', *Except. Child.*, **33**, 13-16.

MORROW, W. R. and WILSON, R. C. (1961) 'Family relations of bright high-achieving and under-achieving high school boys', *Child. Develpmt.*, **32**, 501-10.

MUSSELMAN, J. W. (1942) 'Factors associated with the achievement of high school pupils of superior intelligence', *J. exper. Educ.*, **11**, 53-68.

NASH, R. (1964) 'A study of particular self-perceptions as related to scholastic achievement of junior high school age pupils in a middle class community', *Diss. Abstr.* **24** (9), 3837.

NASON, L. J. (1958) *Academic Achievement of Gifted High School Students.* Univ. Southern California Press.

NATIONAL SOCIETY FOR THE STUDY OF EDUCATION (1924) 'Education of gifted children', Part I, *Yearbook 23.*

NATIONAL SOCIETY FOR THE STUDY OF EDUCATION (1958) 'Education of gifted children', Part II, *Yearbook 57.*

NEVILL, E. M. (1937) 'Brilliant children; with special reference to their particular difficulties', *Brit. J. educ. Psychol.*, **7**, no. 3, 247-58.

NEWLAND, T. E. (1963) 'A critique of research on the gifted', *Except. Child.*, **29**, 393-4.

NORMAN, R. D. (1966) 'The interpersonal values of parents of achieving and non-achieving gifted children', *J. Psychol.*, **64**, 49-57.

NORMAN, R. D., CLARK, B. P. and BESSEMER, D. W. (1962) 'Age, sex, I.Q., and achievement patterns in achieving and non-achieving gifted children', *Except. Child.*, **29**, 116-23.

PARKYN, G. W. (1948) *Children of High Intelligence.* (New Zealand Council for Educational Research.) O.U.P.

PASSOW, A. H. and GOLDBERG, M. L. (1963) 'A study of under-achieving gifted', chap. 7 in *Educating the Academically Able* (eds. L. D. Crow and A. Crow), N.Y., McKay.

PEGNATO, C. V. (1959) 'Identifying the mentally gifted in junior high schools', in *Behavioural Research on Exceptional Children* (eds. S. A. Kirk and B. B. Weiner). Council for Exceptional Children, Washington, D.C.

PERKINS, H. V. (1965) 'Classroom behaviour and under-achievement', *Am. ed. Res. J.*, **2**, no. 1, 10-12.

PETERSON, J. F. (1966) 'A study of the effects of giving teachers personal information about high-ability, low-performing secondary school students', *Diss. Abstr.* **274A**, 263-4

PIERCE, J. V. (1962) 'The bright achiever and under-achiever: a comparison', in Bereday and Lauwerys, Ch. 7, 1962.

PIERCE, J. V. and BOWMAN, P. H. (1960) 'Motivation patterns of superior high school students', *Research Monograph*, U.S. Govmt. Printing Off., No. 2, 33-66.

PRINGLE, M. L. KELLMER (1965a) *Deprivation and Education.* Longmans.

PRINGLE, M. L. KELLMER, ed. (1965b) *Investment in Children.* Longmans.

PRINGLE, M. L. KELLMER (1966) *Social Learning and its Measurement.* Longmans.

PRINGLE, M. L. KELLMER, BUTLER, N. R. and DAVIE, R. (1966) *11,000 Seven-Year-Olds.* Longmans.

PRINGLE, M. L. KELLMER (1967) *Adoption—Facts and Fallacies.* Longmans in association with the National Bureau for Co-operation in Child Care.

RADIN, S. S. and MASLING, J. (1963) 'Tom: a gifted under-achieving child', *J. Child. Psychol. Psychiat.*, **4**, 183-97.

RAPH, J. B., GOLDBERG, M. L. and PASSOW, A. H. (1966) *Bright Under-Achievers.* N.Y., Teachers' College Press.

RAMASESHAN, P. H. (1957) 'Social and emotional adjustment of the gifted', *Dissert. Abstr.* **17**, 1267-8.

ROE, A. (1953) *The Making of a Scientist.* N.Y., Dodd, Mead.

SANFORD, E. G. (1952) 'The bright child who fails', *Understanding Children*, **21**, 85-8.

SCHACHTER, S. (1963) 'Birth order, eminence and higher education', *Am. Soc. Rev.*, **28**, 757-768.

SCHONELL, F. J. (1942; 4th edn, 1949) *Backwardness in the Basic Subjects.* Oliver & Boyd.

SHAW, M. C. and BROWN, D. J. (1957) 'Scholastic under-achievement of bright college students', *Personnel and Guidance J.*, **36**, 195-9.

SHAW, M. C. and McCUEN, J. T. (1960) 'The onset of academic under-achievement in bright children', *J. ed. Psychol.*, **51**, 103-9

SHERTZER, B., ed. (1960) *Working with Superior Students.* Science Res. Ass., Chicago.

SHOUKSMITH, G. and TAYLOR, J. W. (1964) 'The effect of counselling on the achievement of high-ability pupils', *Brit. J. ed. Psychol.*, **34**, no. 1, 51-7.

STRANG, R. M. (1956) 'Counsellor's contribution to guidance of the gifted, the under-achiever and the retarded', *Personnel and Guidance J.*, **34**, 494-7.

SUMPTION, M. R. and LUECKING, E. M. (1960) *Education of the Gifted.* N.Y., Ronald Press Co.

TERMAN, L. M., ed. (1925) *Genetic Studies of Genius*, vols. 1-5. Stanford Univ. Press.

TERMAN, L. M. and ODEN, M. (1947) *The Gifted Child Grows Up.* Stanford Univ. Press.

TERMAN, L. M. *et al.* (1930) *The Promise of Birth.* Stanford Univ. Press.

THOM, D. A. and NEWELL, N. L. (1945) 'Hazards of the high I.Q.', *Mental Hygiene*, **29**, 61-77.

TORRANCE, E. P. (1960) ed. *Talent and Education* (Papers presented at the 1958 Conference on Gifted Children). University of Minnesota Press.

TORRANCE, E. P. and STROM, R. D., eds. (1965) *Mental Health and Achievement*, chaps. 25, 27 and 33.

TRAPP, E. P. and HIMELSTEIN, P., ed. (1962) *Readings on the Exceptional Child*. Methuen.

TRILLINGHAM, C. C. and BONSALL, M. R. (1963) 'The gifted under-achiever', in *Educating the Academically Able*, chap. 6 (eds. L. D. Crow and A. Crow). N.Y., McKay.

WALL, W. D. (1960) 'Highly intelligent children', *Educ. Res.* **2**, pt. 1, 101-10 and pt. 2, 207-17.

WILSON, F. T. (1949) 'Survey of educational provision for young gifted children in the United States, and of studies and problems related thereto', *J. Genet. Psychol.*, **75**, no. 1, 3-19.

WILSON, R. C. (1955) 'The under-educated; how we have neglected the bright child', *Atlantic Monthly*, **195**, no. 5, 60-2.

WITTY, P. (1951) *The Gifted Child*. D. C. Heath.

WONDERLY, D. M. and FLEMING, E. S. (1965) 'Under-achievement and the intelligent creative child', *Except. Child.*, **31**, 405-9.

WORCESTER, D. A. (1956) *The Education of Children of above Average Intelligence*. Univ. of Nebraska Press.

ZWEIG, F. (1961) *The worker in an Affluent society*. Heinemann.

Author Index

Subject Index